IN THE
ROOM
···WE···
SHARE

BOOKS BY LOUIS SIMPSON

Poetry

The Arrivistes: Poems 1940–49
Good News of Death and Other Poems
A Dream of Governors
At the End of the Open Road
Selected Poems
Adventures of the Letter I
Searching for the Ox
Caviare at the Funeral
The Best Hour of the Night
People Live Here: Selected Poems 1949–83
Collected Poems
In the Room We Share

Literary Criticism

James Hogg: A Critical Study
Three on the Tower: The Lives and Works of Ezra Pound,
    T. S. Eliot and William Carlos Williams
A Revolution in Taste: Studies of Dylan Thomas, Allen
    Ginsberg, Sylvia Plath and Robert Lowell
A Company of Poets
The Character of the Poet

Other

Riverside Drive (novel)
An Introduction to Poetry
North of Jamaica (autobiography)
Selected Prose

IN THE ROOM WE SHARE

· LOUIS · SIMPSON

PARAGON HOUSE ▪ NEW YORK

First edition, 1990

Published in the United States by
Paragon House
90 Fifth Avenue
New York, NY 10011

Library of Congress Cataloging-in-Publication Data
Simpson, Louis Aston Marantz, 1923–
        In the room we share / Louis Simpson.
                p.   cm.
        ISBN 1-55778-261-X
        I. Title.
    PS3537.I75I6   1990
    811'.54—dc20   89-38129
                                                        CIP

The paper used in this publication meets the minimum
requirements of
American National Standard for Information
Sciences—Permanence of Paper
for Printed Library Materials, ANSIZ39.48–1984.

Designed by Kathy Kikkert
Manufactured in the United States of America

ACKNOWLEDGMENTS

The poems were first published in the following magazines.

Caliban: "Pursuit of Happiness."
Columbia College Today: "Car Trouble."
The Gettysburg Review: "Santa Monica Boulevard."
Harvard Magazine: "Copyboy," "Reilly's Wonder."
The Hudson Review: "Words" (originally "A Visitor"), "Publishing Days," "His Funny Valentine," "The Magic Carpet," "The Flaubert Pavilion," "The Naturalist and the Volcano."
Ironwood: "Lifers."
The Kenyon Review: "Herons and Water Lilies."
The Missouri Review: "Summer Comes to the Three Villages."
The New Criterion: "Another Boring Story," "White Oxen," "The Rise," "Sea of Grass," "Trouble."
The Ohio Review: "Drugstore Nights," "Neighbors" (first version), "On a Painting by Jimmy Ernst."
Pequod: "A Fuse Link."
Poetry: "Friends," "O What Can Ail Thee, Knight at Arms?", "The People Next Door."
Poetry East: "The Peace March."
Present Tense: "Silence."
Raccoon: " 'Mad' Murray," "Waiting in the Service Station."
Sequoia: "Saudi Arabia."
Southern Humanities Review: "A Bramble Bush."

The Southern Review: "Neptune's Daughter," "The Book of the Opera," "Colonial Education," "Jabez," "Riverside Drive," "Volksgrenadiers," "Villa Rosalinda."

Tar River Poetry: "His and Hers," "It Figures," "Neighbors" (the present version).

The Virginia Quarterly Review: "Numbers and Dust."

Witness: "Harry and Grace."

The World & I: "Café de la Paix" (originally "With Memory. And With Love."), "Personals," "The Bazuft."

"Working Late" is reprinted from *Caviare at the Funeral* by permission of Franklin Watts.

"Villa Selene" was first published in *The Hudson Review.*

For Miriam my love,
who shares my life and work.

CONTENTS

THE OTHER

JAMAICAN

NEPTUNE'S DAUGHTER

I liked stories about America . . .
How the man came into the room
where she sat sewing buttons
and asked if any young ladies
would like to be in motion pictures.

When one of the leading actresses
refused to jump from a bridge
she took her place, jumped in,
and played the part of drowning
to perfection—she couldn't swim.

After that she took swimming lessons,
and came to Jamaica with Annette Kellerman
and her troupe of bathing beauties.
That was where the story stopped
and real life would begin:

a crow flying in circles,
the bray of a mule, bark of a dog,
a voice calling in the lane,
and the breeze that came from the sea
rustling the leaves on the veranda.

THE BOOK OF THE OPERA

The Victor Book of the Opera
had pictures we used to look at.

A man in a helmet and armor
was leaning on a spear
beside a pool or river
and talking to three women
in swimming with no clothes.

This, she said, was how they met.

The Fox Company came to Jamaica
to make a movie, *Neptune's Daughter,*
and stayed at the Myrtle Bank Hotel.

They practiced swimming in the pool,
the breast stroke and the back stroke.
And gentlemen came to look at them.

"But of course we wore clothes.
We were clothed from knee to neck."

The man with a moustache
and a sword, "Don José," looks like him.

This is like her . . . the woman
who is dancing with her shadow.
And again . . . "Pons as Lakmé."

4

COLONIAL EDUCATION

Every Sunday he takes us in his boat
to Port Royal . . . across the harbor
and back. This is boring.

Unless there's an ocean liner
or a warship. The *Rodney*
looks immense . . . the English sailors
leaning on a rail, heroic.

But not when you see them up close
at Bournemouth. They can hardly swim.
They climb on the diving platform
and bellyflop . . . swing on the rings
halfway across, hang there, and drop.

Yet Englishmen are the best
at everything . . . so we are told.
We learn about English history,
and how people living in Manchester
can have a nourishing diet
by "ringing the changes
on pease and beans."

                    I remember the words
exactly. During an exam
the master went out of the room.
Immediately all the desks flew open.

■

Then I had a premonition.
Next day I sat down with the book
and memorized my answers.

Sure enough, we were called up
and stood in a long line
outside Mister Peskett's room.
I heard the thwack of the stick
and the boy before me emerged
pale and trembling. The voice said "Next!"

I went, and gave him all the answers
that he wanted, word for word.
"Hanging," Doctor Johnson said,
"concentrates the mind."

So does the prospect
of six on the arse with a stick.

JABEZ

I am walking in a moonlit lane.
And now I can see our fence,
the streetlight, and a shining
hollow. As I come near
I whistle a tune from the movie.

But the man who is lying there
stands up and has his say:
"My name is Jabez. You knew me.
I lived on the edge of the gully.
On the last night of the hurricane

I went outside. It was black
as pitch, black as the Devil.
I fell into rushing water
and my drowned body floated
here, to stay at your house.

What are you going to make of me
in years to come? Will you talk
of the poverty and injustice
that forced poor black people
to live on the edge of a gully?

Don't, man! Don't try to be political.
Talk about me,
about a bundle of rags
covered with a sheet of iron,
and a pair of naked footsoles."

SILENCE

My brother, in the room we share,
is reading *Physical Culture*
and *How to Win Friends and Influence People.*
He and our stepmother Amy
aren't on speaking terms. She hates him.
Meals take place in silence
and no one comes to the house.

"Breathes there the man, with soul so dead,
Who never to himself hath said,
        This is my own, my native land!"

Yes, Walter, there breathes.
I recall the curse you uttered
on expatriates. The "wretch,"
though he may have power
and "pelf," whatever that means,
is "concentred all in self."

Who has not seen you on Princes Street
in kilt and sporran, the regalia
of a patriot and family man . . .
genius of the tweed shops,
the shops selling cairngorms
or a knife to put in your sock?

But remember that everyone
hasn't had your advantages.

And what is our nation?
The place where we were born
or the one that permits us to live?

WORDS

Words are chalked on the blackboard
under a heading: "Trends:
INDIVIDUALIZE
PRIVATIZE
DEBUREAUCRATIZE."

I read poems and answer questions:
"What's your favorite rock group?" . . .
from parted lips, the breath of Spring,
shining eyes fixed on me.

I admit my ignorance of music,
and some exchange glances.
What can he have to tell us
we'd ever want to listen to?

"DEREGULATE
DECENTRALIZE (LOCALIZE)
PUBLICIZE"

"What made you want to be a writer?"

Summer, the sea rolling in . . .
I had just changed for a swim
and walked from the lockers
when a girl came toward me . . .
gray eyes, long golden hair.
Her eyes met mine and stayed

and I felt a blow that took my senses
away. They flew and clung to her,
to her every look and word
and every movement of a limb.

I dreamed through my adolescence
and thought and wrote about her.

That's how poetry begins:
in youth, with a vision of beauty.
Read Dante, *La Vita Nuova.*
But now I have to catch my plane.
It's been good . . .

　　　　　　　　For God's sake, use your brains!
God knows you'll need to
in a world that uses words like
DEINSTITUTIONALIZE
BUSINESSIZE
VOLUNTEERIZE (OR POLITICALIZE).

I'll just give the blackboard
a quick wipe before I go.

VILLA ROSALINDA

She took the Clipper to New York.

At first Madame wouldn't see her.
"What's she doing here?
She's supposed to be in Caracas."

But she persisted, and finally
Madame relented. "Madame,"
she said, "there's a whole new territory.
You ought to be represented.
Give me an exclusive contract."

And they did, and she went there
and opened a branch of the company,
carrying the boxes herself
up three flights of stairs.

In a few years
she owned a building, a showplace,
across from the American Embassy.
And they tried to break the contract,
but she hired the best lawyers
and beat them.

                    She married again,
an Italian, and when she retired
went to live in his *paèse.*
They bought a villa and named it

Rosalinda. Twenty-five acres
of the best vineyard in Tuscany,
and a pool you could hold Olympics in.

She lived like a contessa
with a cook, a maid, a chauffeur,
and a gardener. Not to mention
the *contadini* . . . farmers
who lived on the estate.

Sometimes a falling leaf or twig
would quiver the surface
of the pool, and the reflection
of the cypresses and walls
and windows would break
into pieces,

and come together again.

WORKING LATE

A light is on in my father's study.
"Still up?" he says, and we are silent,
looking at the harbor lights,
listening to the surf
and the creak of coconut boughs.

He is working late on cases.
No impassioned speech! He argues from evidence,
actually pacing out and measuring,
while the fans revolving on the ceiling
winnow the true from the false.

Once he passed a brass curtain rod
through a head made out of plaster
and showed the jury the angle of fire—
where the murderer must have stood.
For years, all through my childhood,
if I opened a closet . . . bang!
There would be the dead man's head
with a black hole in the forehead.

All the arguing in the world
will not stay the moon.
She has come all the way from Russia
to gaze for a while in a mango tree
and light the wall of a veranda,
before resuming her interrupted journey
beyond the harbor and the lighthouse

at Port Royal, turning away
from land to the open sea.

Yet, nothing in nature changes, from that day to this,
she is still the mother of us all.
I can see the drifting offshore lights,
black posts where the pelicans brood.

And the light that used to shine
at night in my father's study
now shines as late in mine.

RIVERSIDE DRIVE

I have been staring at a sentence
for fifteen minutes. The mind
was not made for social science.

I take my overcoat and go.

Night has fallen on Riverside Drive . . .
the sign for Spry shining
across the Hudson: "Spry for Frying ****
for Baking."

I am thinking of Rilke
and "Who if I cried would hear me
among the angelic orders?"

It seems that we are here to say
names like "Spry" and "Riverside Drive" . . .
to carry the names of places
and things with us, into the night

glimmering with stars and constellations.

"MAD" MURRAY

"Mad" Murray Kadish,
Nick d'Amato, Alfred Dubitch,
Murray Chubinsky, and Saul . . .

They used to take the IRT
downtown every Saturday night
and meet at the Hotel Diplomat.

Why the Diplomat? I passed it recently:
the kind of old hotel that's used now
for housing welfare recipients.

There was Lefty Louie, Nori,
Chink the Knife—named after a gangster—
and the one they called Red Ann.

"Mad" Murray was always the first
up the stairs and running across Broadway.
"What are you guys waiting for? Come on!"

DRUGSTORE NIGHTS

Dipping its beak in a glass . . .
It swings back, oscillates wildly,
then begins lowering its beak
once more, going through the cycle.
There was a bird like that in the window
of the store where Al used to work:
Whelan's, on Broadway, just above Times Square.

Al was a certified pharmacist
though I never saw him fill a prescription.
He'd be attending to a customer,
selling cosmetics, toilet articles,
a pair of nail scissors . . .
barely acknowledging my arrival
with a nod, the engaged professional.

When he'd rung up the sale
he'd come around the counter. "How's it going
up at Columbia?" "Fine," I'd say.

We talked about all the fun I must be having.
Or perhaps some famous personality
had come into the store that day:
Ethel Merman or Billy Rose.
He had sold aspirin and Pepto-Bismol
to some of the biggest names.

Odd people came into the store
late at night: an old woman
in ratty mink, who'd been on the radio
in the thirties, and now was living,
if you could call it that, in one of the fleabags
off Broadway. Al kept an eye on her—
that was the type that went in for shoplifting.

■

It was a big difference, going from Whelan's
with its bright fluorescent interior
to Al's house out in Brooklyn.
The street was poorly lighted.

Al's wife was a *baleboosteh,* the homemaker
whose price, the Bible tells us, is above rubies,
but fat with her own cooking—
not at all like the chorus girls
who came into the drugstore,
and beautiful faces gazing at you
from the covers of magazines.

She is standing over a platter
of angel food cake and whipped cream,
the leftover dessert,
gobbling with the serving spoon.
Her skirt, hiked up behind, reveals
huge thighs bulging above rolled stockings.

I close my eyes, then, keeping them averted,
back silently out of the room.

■

The bird dipping its beak in a glass
reminded me. I ought to pay Al a visit.

He was at Mount Sinai Hospital.
On the way over I made some purchases:
Tic Tacs, a roll of Lifesavers
in different flavors, the latest issue of *Playboy*.

He looked surprised—we hadn't been
close. My strange vocation,
poetry, made the whole family nervous.

I gave him the packets of candy
and *Playboy*. He looked at the table of contents
as though it were some sort of test.
We talked and ran out of words.
Then the nurse came and helped him from the bed
to a wheelchair, and carried him away
for more x-rays.

                    I never saw him again,
but I can see the drugstore as clear as day
with its green fluorescent lighting,
shelves lined with bottles and containers,
the display of nail polish, array
of toothbrushes in colorful Lucite,
and the magazines, all the shining bodies and faces.

NUMBERS AND DUST

All day we were training in dust.
At night we returned to barracks
worn out, too tired to say anything.

On weekends we traveled long distances
to Fort Worth, Austin, San Antonio,
looking for excitement, walking up and down
with all the other enlisted men,
trying to pick up a shop girl
or waitress hurrying home.

No luck that way, so we'd split up
and agree to meet back at the depot.

■

Now you're by yourself, on Vine Street
or Magnolia, gazing at sprinklers,
a bicycle lying in the drive.

A curtain moves as you pass . . . some old lady.

Then there are bigger houses, with lawns and
    gardens:
English Tudor, a French château,
Bauhaus. The rich like to shop around.

■

I am a guest years later
in one of those houses.

                    Looking through a window
at some trees, I ask their names.
"Flowering judas, golden rain tree,
ceniza . . . that's very Texan."

And the birds picking at berries?
Waxwings. They get drunk, she says.

In the room behind me Isaac Singer
is talking about golems, things like men
created out of numbers and dust.

                 ■

Two rabbis once made a golem
and sent it to Rabbi Zera
who tried to engage it in conversation.
But the golem spoke not a word.
Finally he said, "You must have been made
by the numbers. Return to your dust."

I think I can see one now,
standing by the gate,
in the uniform of an enlisted man.

It stands looking up at me
for a few moments, then turns away
in silence, returning to dust.

VOLKSGRENADIERS

A tank comes jingling up.
The crew climb out with a dixie
and gasoline. Brewing up.

When the first shell comes in . . .
"Cheerio, Yank!" and push off.
Shell upon shell cracks.

When night falls and the moon
glimmers in leaves and branches
the Volksgrenadiers sit up.

One gathers his intestines . . .
they're slippery and keep escaping.
The other with his one hand

feels in the dirt around him.
"Meinen Arm . . . Er hat eine Tätowierung
mit zwei Herzen . . . 'Fritz und Elsa.' "

CAFÉ DE LA PAIX

Peace, in all your avenues
new galaxies are shining . . .
Chocolats Lindt   Montres Kody
Coryse   Salome   Parfums
"Tourism," a sign announces, "in Germany."

There's Saint-Germain . . . the café
where for a year I was a student.
I used to know these streets
and windows, all the stuffed animals
in Rue du Bac, the buffalo,
lion, hyena, and baby camel . . .
and would often stop to gaze
in the Seine, at the fire brigade
still caressing their *Souqui*
though all her brass and varnish glitters.

Les Halles where we used to eat onion soup
is now a huge glass arboretum
where discotheques and boutiques blossom.
The young hang out there, in jeans . . .
unisex. The more outrageous
shave their heads, leaving a strip
down the middle, dyed orange or green.
That is the latest thing, a "mohican."

But the women around Saint-Denis
stick to skirts and high heels.
Plus ça change . . . their clients are sentimental.

HERONS AND WATER LILIES

I am walking behind three men,
obviously undergraduates,
who are talking in loud voices.
Why do they have to read Plato?

They speak of the opportunities
in medicine and law . . . in computers.
Who cares about Shakespeare?
What's Hecuba to them?

■

The most brilliant undergraduate
at Columbia when I was there
was a man named Carlos Fonseca.
Charlie came from South America . . .
Paraguay or Uruguay . . .
exotic in any case.

When I came back from the war
I found that most of my classmates
had somehow managed to avoid it.
Two were full-fledged psychiatrists,
one making a name in physics.
Charlie was taking a PhD—
also pinch-hitting for a professor,
a famous man who was often absent.
Charlie would take his classes.
His lectures, I was told, were brilliant.

But a rule said, seven years
to finish the degree, or else . . .
He tried, but as often happens
with lecturers, he couldn't write.
That year three instructors were fired.
One threw himself from a roof,
one went into business, selling menswear,
and Charlie found another position.

■

A writer once made a remark
I have never forgotten:
"Imagine a scholar specializing
in the Renaissance, who finds himself
teaching at a state university
in the Midwest. Think what that man
must have to reconcile."

This was the very fellow.
I could imagine him growing up
in South America. I visualized
a Spanish villa, tropical flowers,
servants. An illustrious father
in the government. A mother
who, as a girl, studied singing
in Europe, and then was married
to this God-forsaken country.
Carlos was her darling . . . the best food,
best schools. I could see her handkerchief
waving as her son took ship

for North America. Carlos's father
wasn't at the dock—he'd been shot.
As I said, an exotic background.

And now what did I see?
The house he was in faced a cornfield.
Nothing but telephone wires
and crows.

We had dinner that night
with a dean who treated Charlie
with what I can only describe
as contempt. When Charlie launched
into the kind of brilliant talk
that held us spellbound at Columbia
the dean interrupted rudely
to ask who wanted more soup.

There were some faculty members
who'd been invited, and their wives.
When Charlie enthused over Plato
I saw them winking and giggling.
Charlie, apparently, was the faculty fool.

■

I never saw him again.
But one day when I went to my office
people were staring at a poster,
the picture of a man with a beatific smile.

EXPLORE THE UNIVERSE OF SELF
WITH VADYAMIHALY
—Dr. Charles Fonseca

Set forth on the Way (Kenshō)
and be free of the bonds of spiritual ignorance.

GOALS OF THE KENSHŌ PROGRAM:

To contact my students from past lives and achieve
their liberation.

To meet individuals who are burdened with
difficulties and set their feet in the path to
Self-Knowledge, Enlightenment, and Truth.

"That art Thou!"

VADYAMIHALY—EXPERIENCE:

1465–1493   Zen Master, Osaka
1556–1579   Professor of Theology, Salamanca
1660–1693   Professor of Philosophy, Heidelberg
1786–1807   Head of the Monastery, Lhasa
1948–   Self-Liberated Spiritual Instructor

EVERY YEAR A CERTAIN NUMBER OF
APPLICANTS ARE ADMITTED
to the Kenshō Program. To apply for admission, write

THE VADYAMIHALY INSTITUTE, MESA,
ARIZONA

■

When the view from the window
was a stubble field and crows . . .

as he slaved in the system
from time to time he would pause
to gaze at a Chinese screen:
a man fishing in a river
among herons and water lilies.

Then Inspiration came.
From her long golden hair
to her feet *O dea certe,*
she came toward him carrying
the torch of an idea.
In that hour he died to the university
and was reborn as Vadyamihaly.

"I must Create a System
or be enslaved to another Man's,"
Blake says (O that smiling, damned
Dean of so-called Humanities!).

           People are reborn
every day. And what is reality
after all? Even Shakespeare
who knew more about life than anyone
at the end has Prospero say
life is a dream.

Everything we see and use
was once imagined: the chair
I'm sitting on, window
I look out of . . . trees and roofs
have been images in a stream
in which an old man fishes.

PUBLISHING DAYS

Sitting at a desk with my feet up
on the bottom drawer, reading manuscripts,

I have a vision of an author, in his underwear
at the typewriter. Through a window
come noises: boys playing ball, the diastole
of traffic. But he is oblivious,
typing away faster than I can read.

Now and then I leave my desk
and stroll about . . . look out the window
to the Hudson, where the ocean liners
tie up: the *Elizabeth,*
the *New Amsterdam,* the *Ile de France* . . .
and sit down again. The work is pleasant,
undemanding, and underpaid.

■

I go to literary gatherings
where editors rub elbows with authors
and agents. There are familiar faces:
Mailer, Styron, Baldwin, Bellow,
and many that have since disappeared.

The room is filled with smoke, a hubbub
of talk about paperback sales
and Hollywood contracts. The door keeps opening
with more and more crowding to get in,
like the cabin scene in *A Night at the Opera.*

30

■

Sometimes I take the train
to Old Greenwich, Connecticut,
where the head editor has his house.
There the party is continuing . . .
more novelists, more literary agents,
and some of J. B.'s more personable neighbors:
a corporation lawyer, say, or psychiatrist.

We play games like Twenty Questions . . .
a game, I recall, in which you choose
one of the people in the room
and they all guess, by asking questions,
which one it is. Questions such as,
"If this person were an automobile
what kind of automobile would it be?"
Frequently this leads to a discussion
of the person's character . . . sometimes flattering
and sometimes, definitely, not.

■

One weekend there is a hurricane
and flood warning. Cars come up Old Clubhouse
    Road
from the beach, honking their horns.
But J. B.'s house stands on higher ground
and, he assures us, we are in no danger.

With time things that never happened
seem as real as things that did.
The house is floating out on the Sound

with lighted windows, and a voice
from inside it, faintly heard,
is asking, "If this person were a vegetable
what kind of vegetable would it be?"

HIS FUNNY VALENTINE

He said, "I'd like to be a beautiful woman."

I was taken aback.
It sounded, and still sounds, most unlikely.
He was extremely attractive to women.
If you went with Mike Donovan to a party
or entered a restaurant, women would glance up,
see his face, and keep on staring.

I said, "Like Marilyn Monroe?"
I said that wanting to be someone else
was the same as wishing you were dead.

■

A woman said, "Tell me about Donovan.
You're his friend."
I said, "Mike's a drunk."
"Not that," she said, "something significant."

I told her about the affair
Mike had been having with Penny Baker.
"O that," she said. "He told me about it.
It's all over."

I might as well have tried to reason
with the 7th Cavalry charging down the valley.

33

■

He introduced me to Penny
in the White Horse. She was with her husband.
Later, in the course of conversation
something came up that required her
to open her shirt and show us her breasts . . .
like lilies, with nipples like tea roses.
"Come on, Penny," said her husband, "cover up."

That same night Mike came over
to drink and talk. I left him to it
and went to bed. Some time later
I was wakened by a sound.
He was still there, on the floor, passed out,
with the phonograph set on automatic
playing "My Funny Valentine" over and over.

■

I might have told her he'd been writing a novel
ever since I'd known him, that he had a contract
with Simon and Schuster, but never wrote a page.

There was a new postwar generation
of young novelists. Every few weeks
there'd be a new first-novel sensation.

At the time there was a run on titles
that told the reader to do something:
to *Lie Down in Darkness* and *Go Tell It on the
Mountain.*

Mike had a title for his:
Do Not Pass Go, Do Not Collect $200.
But, as far as I know, it never came to anything.

∎

Though a man who saw him in Italy
years later, shortly before he died,
said he was still writing . . . on Janiculum
with a view of Rome through the pines.
He was living with an Italian woman.

It was a far cry from the Village
and Albany where he grew up,
a boy with a taste for books
and baseball. He could still recite batting averages.

Later, when he went to the university,
it was jazz. And still, occasionally,
he wrote on jazz for the *Times.*

∎

Speaking of *The New York Times,*
there was an item about a golfer
who was playing with a metal club
behind a hedge. He fell on his club
and it snapped and went right through him.

Some who were playing the eighteenth hole
that day, close to the hedge, heard screams,
but they thought it was peacocks.
Peacocks were one of the features of the area.

That night when I met Mike for dinner
we had both seen it. I quoted Robert Frost:
a "design of darkness to appall."
Mike said, Ambrose Bierce. And, of course, he was
    right.

This may have been why we liked each other.
We liked the sound of fate:
a horn heard at a distance
in the Valley of the Shadow.

■

When Mike stuck a knife in Penny
I didn't go to the precinct station
to bail him out—someone else did.
But ever since I've had an idea

of what it's like: a woman in a yellow wig,
a purple skirt, and heels like stilettos;
a pickpocket; a cripple
arrested for indecent exposure;

the naked light; the crack in the wall
that loops like the Mississippi at Vicksburg;
the shadow of the cockroach
under the baseboard, lurking, gathering his nerve.

FRIENDS

Even after J. B. left and went to a better house
I still sat there reading manuscripts.

Lindsay: A Romance of Old Virginia . . .
There'd be a long red hair
or else a soup or jam stain.
I envisioned her in a dressing gown
typing away. Then she'd pause
to eat jam out of the jar with a spoon.

Waycross, by a retired businessman . . .
When I said that we couldn't publish it
a tear came to each eye and ran slowly down.

■

"You want to leave," Mike said.
"Find another occupation.
There is a tide in the affairs of men
which, taken at the flood, leads on to fortune;
omitted, all the voyage of their lives
is bound in shallows and in miseries."

"Life," I said.
"All the voyage of their life."

His mouth was full of steak.
He stopped chewing. "Tell me," he said,
"have you thought of being a professor?"

■

I left publishing and went into teaching.
Now I'm surrounded by professors.
They don't believe in experience,
only theory . . . figures of speech.

I prefer the redhaired woman
with her jam jar and her spoon;
the woman with the mating machine;
the man who brings you a manuscript
in a box fastened with a chain.

Irving Berlin has been entering his apartment
for years and stealing his songs.

2

SOMETHING

HUMAN

... but the Dwarf answered: "No,
something human is dearer to me
than the wealth of the world."

Grimm's *Tales*

LIFERS

His hands move with the half wheel
some fractions of an inch. Over to the right

is Huntsville Prison where they hold the rodeo.
"Lifers," he says, "they don't care what they do."

His two sons-in-law are ministers.
One daughter is a ThD, doctor of theology.

■

It is the warm air from the Gulf,
he says, that makes the plane unstable.

It is the warm air from the gulf,
a poet said, at the bottom of myself . . .

a being made of nothing if that is at all possible.
Perhaps it is of the Void as the void is.

■

The forest we are passing over is a national park
with flora and fauna indigenous to the area.

There is an ivory-billed woodpecker,
"a big feller," fondly, shaping it with his hand.

And still there are those in prison,
lifers . . . they don't care what they do.

THE PEACE MARCH

We are carrying lighted candles.
People have come out of their houses
to watch. Some of them make remarks.

One puts a foot out. I step over.
The two lines slow to a stop
and start again. We almost have to run

to catch up. The woman next to me
has lost one of her contact lenses.
The peace march isn't what it was supposed to be.

Some of the candles have gone out,
and more and more go wandering off
down Cedar and Livingston and Buena Vista.

O WHAT CAN AIL THEE, KNIGHT
AT ARMS?

The day the students were arrested,
"Here you," she said, "answer the phone.
I have to go down the hall.
If a bail-bondsman calls, take the message."

So he went to work for the FSM,
answering the phone, relaying messages,
typing.

"The incarnation of a human soul
in a body, some particular feature,
can blot out the world."

"That's beautiful," she said. "Who wrote it?"

"I did," he said. She was moved.
That was the first time she went to bed with him.

■

But it didn't seem to mean anything—
he was just one of her friends.
She had several: a social worker,
an oboe-player, an artist
who had painted her in the nude.

He said, "You're La Belle Dame Sans Merci."
She said, "What does that mean?"

43

It's a poem, he told her, about a fairy
who takes up with a knight.
He dreams of other men she's had;
they've come to warn him about her,
and he wakes alone on the cold hillside.

I like poetry, she said.
I just don't have the time for it.

■

At night when a foghorn boomed
he imagined a troopship leaving
for Vietnam, men huddled on deck
for a last look at the shore
and the lights of the Bay Area.

He helped to organize a peace march.
The Hell's Angels charged the line
with their motorcycles, breaking arms and legs.

■

He protested and was teargassed,
climbed a fence and was arrested.

Outside the precinct station,
in the streets, life was going on
as usual . . . storekeepers,
pedestrians . . . the green parrot
in its cage at the Pet Emporium.

He walked to Telegraph Avenue
and sat and had a beer.
There were some people he knew
at a table . . . friends of Marilyn.

They said, "Come and join us."
Yes, he thought. I might as well.

SANTA MONICA BOULEVARD

Finding where he keeps things,
tea bags and cups and spoons. . .

On one wall there's a crucifix,
stained dark like the furniture.
Dark and ornate . . . a Spanish atmosphere.

On another wall, newspaper clippings
and photos. One with Marlon Brando,
and several with a woman
I vaguely recognize.
Blonde, a distinctive smile . . .
I've seen her somewhere
in the movies.
Goodfall. That's it. Marilyn Goodfall.

According to a gossip column
his "fiancée." Whaddye know!

■

Banks and automobile showrooms,
a Cadillac with gold-plated hubcaps . . .

A block further on, Mercedes-Benz . . .
"If you don't have cash don't look!"
Do people actually walk around
with $40,000 in their pockets?
In Los Angeles they do.

And here a huge ship's anchor
has fallen out of the sky
to the sidewalk. The *Queen Mary's*
says the plaque. Some p. r. man . . .
"Let's put the *Queen Mary's* anchor
on Santa Monica Boulevard."

But where everything is surprising
or colossal, nothing is.

■

Now I'm on Beverly Drive . . .
fat palm trees alternating with thin
like husbands with dieting wives.

Each house I pass is the facade
for a movie, the imitation
of a palace or a mansion,
a Manderley long ago.

This replica of a church
in thirteenth-century Florence . . .
can anyone really live there?

Each house has its plot of grass
and a warning: "Armed Response."
If you pushed the gate open
and walked up the path
alarms and sirens would go off.

■

I'm waiting for the driver
who's supposed to pick me up.
Nothing on TV but the usual,
so I sit staring at the wall
and its story, *A Star Is Born.*

He lost his job with the studio
and drank, or the other way round,
while she went on to better things,
leaving him to his crucifix
and tea bags, cups and spoons.

Did they part in anger, recriminating?
I like to think, more in sorrow.

No matter. Whatever the story,
the crucifix has to mean something
and so do his newspaper clippings.

CAR TROUBLE

I'm at the service station
in a room with two green chairs,
a magazine table . . . sounds
coming from the work area:
hammering, an electric drill.

I'm not the only customer.
There's a salesman. "You have to have a car,"
he says, "in my line of business."

A good-looking woman enters,
and sits, and has nice knees.
Which reminds him . . . on one of his trips
he met a woman. He used to see her
whenever he was driving through.
He used to drive like a crazy person . . .
looking at his watch,
pulling out of the line,
passing, and cutting back in
just in time.

It couldn't continue.
She was a married woman with kids.

He still has thoughts about her.
They drove to the shore and watched the sunset
and arranged to see each other in Boston.

Have I ever been to Stanky's?
Stanky's Harbor Bar and Restaurant?

No, I say, I haven't,
but I know the kind of place.

PERSONALS

"The breakfront." She touched a switch
and an enormous piece of furniture
lit up. It had glass doors
and shelves lined with glasses and cups.

She walked around turning lights on
and when everything that she owned
was illuminated—the sailing ship,
the shepherdess with her crook and dog—

she removed her coat,
and he saw why she had kept it on
all through dinner. Osteoporosis.

The backbone ending in a hump.
The neck angling from the trunk
like the branch of a dead tree.

■

You'd think he'd have given it up.
Not Sam—he finds it exciting,
writing to "SWF 34,
blonde voluptuous beauty,"
and to "WWF, petite professional."

Driving toward Syosset,
the red taillights of the car in front
floating up and down,

a bright moon casting shadows,
and a woman lying on a cloud.

She likes to dance, but is content
to sit by the fire and read.

THE MAGIC CARPET

1

Every American is a movie critic.
We come by it naturally.
They don't have to teach it in school.

If she slaps him they'll soon kiss.

How to tell a villain . . .
He speaks English correctly,
has a butler and strokes a cat.

Let the people of other nations
make the cars and build cathedrals—
we know how to look at moving pictures.

So when a man named Wachsman phoned
and asked if I'd like to go to Paris
to see a movie and write subtitles
for twenty thousand dollars,
my expenses paid and back . . .

We had lunch the next day with his "associates,"
a Mister Peres and Miss Zigano.
"There's one thing," he said, "you should know.
If we decide to buy the rights
you can't back out later."

The associates looked me over.
I had a vision . . . of a body
surfacing in the East River.
"No," I said, "I won't change my mind."

He leaned across and shook my hand.
"Good."

His sleeves had cuff links.
Not human molars . . . ordinary gold.

2

I flew to Paris first class.
Lots of leg room
and liquor . . . plenty of that.

The hotel I was staying at
was right off the Champs Élysées
and furnished in grand style . . .
high ceilings, crystal chandeliers,
chairs and sofas in red velvet.

My room was on the same grand scale.
A card on the desk informed me
that a refrigerator had been stocked
for my convenience.

Another card . . .
that the Hotel Alexandre III

assured "en exclusivité"
to its clients female and male
the services of Madame Jacqueline Cornu
MASSEUSE-KINÉSITHÉRAPEUTE.

Where was it? I felt along the wall
and a panel opened. There was everything
for my convenience. I filled a glass
with whiskey.

Left a wake-up call,
crawled into bed, and turned out the light.

3

I was on my second cup of coffee
when Wachsman appeared.

How was my flight?
Good. There were two items on my agenda.
I was having lunch with his assistant,
Monique.

And, at five, everybody
would be meeting in his suite.
Then he and Monique would take me to dinner.

Till five then. I took my leave
and walked to the Champs Élysées.

I bought *La Quinzaine* and had an espresso,
looking at the passersby.
I could see myself years ago,
a student enrolled in the course
of Preparation and Perfectionment.

There were a bunch of Americans.
We didn't stay the course . . .
only Sy Coleman. He went into business,
importing, and sends his greetings
every Christmas . . . a picture of himself
smiling, with his wife and kids.
All my other Left Bank friends,
the painter, the composer, the novelist
have disappeared more or less.

I walked to the Rue de Rivoli
and browsed in the English bookstore.

4

Monique was the Parisienne
complete, down to the poodle
that she parked at our feet.

I ordered snails. "That's unusual,"
she said, "for an American."
I told her I'd lived in France

for a year and never tried them
till the night before my ship sailed.
I liked them . . . but then it was too late.

Wachsman—whom she called Bernie—
had wanted us to meet.
What did I think about sex?
The movie I was going to see
was "erotic" . . . I shouldn't be shocked.

I said that it took more than a movie.
I'd had the usual experiences.
Besides, sex didn't seem as important
as it used to. In recent years
I'd found there was nothing better
than a woman you could talk to.

She smiled brightly. "Like the snails."

5

Bernie's partner had flown in
from London . . . one of a new generation
of youthful impresarios.
He managed the Odes of Keats, a rock group.

There were the two French producers,
Monique acting as interpreter.

Bernie introduced me as "the writer,
I'm sure you know his work."

I talked to one of the Frenchmen.
The movie we were going to see
was based on a novel by Jules Romains.
I was discussing Romains's theory
of Unanism when I became aware
that the room had fallen silent
and everyone was listening.
My opinions would be worth money
for the next twenty-four hours.

When I had finished talking . . .
"It's very fine, that," said Monique.

"Your friend," she said to Bernie,
"likes snails. I know a restaurant
where he can have them four different ways."

So we went there, and I ate the quaternion
and drank a carafe of wine.

Bernie and Monique were dancing.
He held her almost formally.
She danced with tosses of her head,
an air of gay abandon.

6

He stood on the embankment
looking down. A train had stopped
and he could see into the dining car . . .
waiters, people sitting at the tables
eating.

"Do you know what it was like
in the Depression? We were hungry.
And here were these rich people,
dressed in fine clothes,
eating all they liked, shoveling food
into their mouths."

There was a little girl
right below him. She took a taste
of something on her plate,
made a face, and pushed it away.
Then she looked up, saw him,
and pointed.

He ran away.
But that dining car made an impression.

"I said to myself, one day
I'm going to eat all I want,
wear good clothes, and see the world.
That's what we're put here for,
to enjoy ourselves," said Bernie Wachsman.

7

The man who wrote the screenplay
insisted on taking me to lunch
at Le Sahara. He was English
but liked his food highly spiced.

Over mounds of couscous
he told me that the "réalisation"
had presented certain difficulties.
For instance, there was a scene
in which a woman seduced the hero
under a table with her feet.

They found a freak in a circus sideshow
who could untie knots with her toes.

But *The Magic Carpet* wasn't pornography.
"You'll see . . . it's on the crest
of a new wave, the erotic."

When the check came he picked it up
with a horrible smile. Two of his teeth
were missing, the rest brown with nicotine.
"This is on me," he said, "you're my guest."

8

Credits rolled. The opening scene . . .
in an office, with stenographers.
Lots of leg shots.

Who was it Mencken called
a garter snapper? Hoffenheimer?
Hoffenheimer should have been here.

This was the seduction scene
the writer described, under the table.
The feet were short and fat.
They curved and wriggled . . .
like the feet of a circus freak.

There was one scene that pretended
to . . . what's it called? Redeeming value.

A poet reclining in a harem
recited some lines about flowers
and clouds, to a bevy of women,
the same who played the stenographers.
They had changed out of their skirts
and garter belts into Turkish costume,
some diaphanous material.

The lights went on. The projectionist
was changing reels. In a flash
Bernie's partner and I
were at his side.

        I said,
"It has nothing to do with the novel,
it's just soft core pornography,

the kind of picture they used to make
years ago in the States. It's terrible.
No one will want to see it."

Bernie turned to his partner.
He said, "I agree. It's no good at all."

We saw it through to the end
where the hero faced a firing squad
and was saved by his fiancée.
Disguised as one of the houri-stenographers
she came flying on a magic carpet.

"It was very amusing, no?" said Monique,
smiling at me.
"Would you like to see it again?
We have the cinema for the afternoon."

No, I said, there was no need,
and she stopped smiling.

9

If the French were disappointed
they didn't show it.

We adjourned to a brasserie
where they spoke of other projects,
talking rapidly, citing figures
in the millions. Francs or dollars?

I didn't ask, for fear of showing
my ignorance.

They spoke of distant places . . .
Luanda, Brasília,
that offered unheard-of opportunities.

Bernie took me to one side.
"These people may approach you
and ask you to work for them
on the movie. What will you say?"

I saw the body in the East River
bumping gently against a pier.
"I'd say no, of course."

Then we went back to the Alexandre
to check out.

He looked at every item.
It's one thing to live on a grand scale,
another to be overcharged.

10

I moved to a hotel I know
on the Left Bank, that charges
twenty-five francs, including breakfast.

Here is my Paris, in these stones
and gutters . . . the smell of bread,
the butcher's, the perfumery,
the jeweler's.

The window of Nérée Boŭbée et Cie.
Naturalistes . . .
the skeleton of a toucan,
skeleton of a monkey,
rib cage of another monkey . . .
not to mention Minéralogie,
Paléontologie, and Pétrographie.

In the Louvre I look at still lifes
by Chardin . . . and the man himself
with his green eyeshade, looking up,
still absorbed . . . in three eggs,
a ceramic bowl,
some object like a ladle,
and a big copper pot.

I go to a play by Molière.

I gaze on the Pont des Arts
upstream at the island city
like a dragonfly on her bridges . . .
in the midst a single spire reaching
to the pearl-gray sky.

11

I heard from Bernie again
years later . . . that is, from his lawyer.
He phoned to say that Bernie
was being sued for divorce.

If I were asked about his relations
with a woman in Paris . . . Monique Benayoun . . .
what would I say?

I said, that I had seen her
at a conference in his suite,
then the three of us went to dinner.
It all seemed perfectly innocent.

I heard the voice of the lawyer
relaying this information
to a voice in the background . . .

a voice that spoke of flying
to four-star hotels and restaurants . . .
of deals in movies, in diamonds,
in machine guns . . .
in anything but this silence,
this green wall of leaves,
and two azaleas.

What color are they?
I ask. "Fuchsia," she says.

She helps me with my writing.
Without her I'd probably be
at the bottom of the East River
with my feet in a concrete block.

A perfect natural specimen
for Nérée Boŭbée et Cie,
with the "hippocampe," a sea horse,
and "siponelle," large worm.

ANOTHER BORING STORY

Chekhov has "A Boring Story"
about a professor.
The old man's wife and children
don't understand him and don't care.

His wife's only concern is
to marry off their daughter
to this blockhead, a nonentity.
So the old man goes on a journey
to investigate, find out what he can
about their future son-in-law . . .
and finds himself in a hotel room
in a strange town, wondering
how on earth life brought him there.

He has a friend, a young woman.
They're not lovers . . . loving friends.
She had an affair that turned sour
and now she's at loose ends.
She asks him what to do, what to live for,
and he has nothing to say to her,
not a word. That's the end of the story.

Here's another boring story about a professor.
Years ago he embarked on an affair
with a young woman. It became a scandal.
His wife threw him out,

then she took him back. The young woman
tried to kill herself, I'm told.

I see them fairly often.
He and I talk about literature
and what's wrong with the country
while his wife knits or does some ironing.

I find myself looking out the window
or at the walls. Some surrealist
recommends staring at a wall
till something unusual happens . . .
an arm protruding from the wall.

He mixes drinks, she lays out cheese-dip.
Then the children come running in,
streaked with dirt from wherever they've been.
They make for the cheese-dip,
stick their fingers in and dabble.

I've seen them at the table.
They snatch the meat from the plate
with their hands.

She smiles at her little savages.
One thing's sure: she's not raising her children
to be members of any faculty.

HARRY AND GRACE

I used to go over to the Fergusons
on weekends.
There were a number of people,
Harry and Grace's friends.
We'd sit around drinking and talking
about politics or lawn fertilizer.

Then Harry would get out his tools
for the outdoor barbecue.

This was before Grace left.
I saw her afterwards in New York.
She had an apartment on the East Side
with a view from the picture window
like a picture in a coloring book:
a car, a truck, a tugboat, a helicopter.

It wasn't just the novel
she had felt compelled to write. . . .
It wasn't just Harry
with his baseball statistics
and his barbecue pit and bug zapper,
but the whole fucking scene in the Hamptons.

She had learned to use four-letter words . . .
apparently from her friend,
some sort of commercial artist.
We talked about living in New York

and he said that the streets were safe.
You just had to carry a knife.
It didn't have to have a long blade . . .
two and a half inches.
He took a knife out of his pocket
and held it at arm's length.
He had long arms I noticed.

It's tempting to see them as types
and hold him up to ridicule . . .
in his chef's apron and hat
sprinkling *Wizard* on the charcoal.
The apron has a saying on it. . . .

But people aren't the whole story.
There's an open field . . . the beach
just down the road.

Now and then
geese fly up from the ocean,
follow in a straight line,
honking . . . change direction,
and fly inland.

The sunset
is lining a cloud with gold,
flashing from a window on the headland.

"Come and get it!" Harry calls.
I get myself a paper plate
and take my place in line.

THE PEOPLE NEXT DOOR

He isn't a religious man.
So instead of going to church
on Sunday they go to sea.

They cruise up and down,
see the ferry coming from Bridgeport
to Green Harbor, and going back
from Green Harbor to Bridgeport . . .
and all the boats there are.
The occasional silent fisherman . . .
When the kids start to get restless
he heads back to shore.

I hear them returning
worn out and glad to be home.
This is as close to being happy
as a family ever gets.
I envy their content. And yet
I've done that too, and know
that no hobby or activity
distracts one from thinking
forever. Every human being
is an intellectual more or less.

I too was a family man.
It was a phase I had to go through.
I remember tenting in the Sierras,
getting up at dawn to fly cast.

I remember my young son
almost being blown off the jetty
in Lochalsh. Only the suitcase
he was carrying held him down.
The same, at Viareggio,
followed me into the sea
and was almost swept away by the current.

These are the scenes I recall
rather than Christmas and Thanksgiving.
My life as the father of a family
seems to have been a series
of escapes, not to mention illnesses,
confrontations with teachers,
administrators, police.
Flaubert said, "They're in the right,"
looking at a bourgeois family,
and then went back happily
to his dressing gown and pipe.

Yes, I believe in the family . . .
next door. I rejoice
at their incomings and outgoings.
I am present when Betty
goes out on her first date.
I hear about Joey's being chosen
for the team. I survive the takeover
of the business, and the bad scare
at the doctor's.
I laugh with them that laugh
and mourn with them that mourn.

I see their lights, and hear a murmur
of voices, from house to house.

It gives me a strange feeling
to think how far they've come
from some far world to this,
bending their necks to the yoke
of affection.

              And that one day,
with a few simple words
and flowers to keep them company
they'll return once more to the silence
out there, beyond the stars.

HOMELAND

Thought, sweet magnet
that takes us away from everything . . .
moon in the dark evening, large and
   clear,
more our homeland than the world!

Juan Ramón Jiménez

COPYBOY

On the *New York Evening News*
there was a copyboy named Jim
we all thought simpleminded.

He would bring you an article:
"U.S. Sinks 45
Small Wicker Boats Near Danang."
"How do they know?" he'd ask.
"Forty-five . . . Did they count them?"

One day Jim suddenly quit.
I talked to a woman in Personnel
and she said he gave no reason.

Since then I've often had occasion
to think about him: "Sikhs Halt Bus
and Kill 13 Hindus."

"Murder Suspect Morales" . . .
the picture of a curlyhaired youth
in handcuffs. "What does it mean?"
Jim asks. "Why is he laughing?"

SAUDI ARABIA

He worked for an oil company
and was flying to St. Paul
to see his children by his first wife.
He had recently married again
and showed me her picture:
a fair young woman in shorts.
She was English and liked to play tennis.

For years he had lived alone,
going to bed with them—
a nod to the airline stewardess.
His father said to him, "One day
you'll wake up next to one
and find that you've bought her,
and be sorry the rest of your life."

"Look," he said, opening his briefcase,
"if they like you in Saudi Arabia
they will give you anything."
And he took out a golden chain
from which hung tablets of gold,
each with its weight inscribed in ounces.
And he showed me a golden ring.

REILLY'S WONDER

By Lough Ree in Roscommon
there's a small, middle-aged man
named Reilly who hires out boats.

He showed me how to tie a fly,
but for all his expertise at fishing
he seemed to place no store by it.
What he wanted to talk about was women.
Were there many in the States?

I said there were. Then he wanted to know,
could you ask them to go out with you?
Yes, I said. And how much would that cost?

I told him. He was silent,
but not, I thought, discouraged.
Though the likelihood of his ever going
to America was small . . .

To think that somewhere in the world
are women who will go out with you
if you ask them, and not change at sight
into an otter or a bird!

PURSUIT OF HAPPINESS

I tried TM, Transcendental Meditation.
You waited, with the fruit and flower
you'd been told to bring.
There was incense and Indian music.

Then you were told to go in.
A young woman in a granny gown
beckoned you to come near.
She took the fruit and flower
and whispered in your ear
a word . . . to be said silently
to yourself, over and over,
and never divulged to anyone.

I soon grew bored with TM,
and so was the rest of the country.
Then the rage for physical fitness started . . .
people running around in the park
or joining a gymnasium.

I joined Jack LaLanne. Three,
maybe four times a week,
I rode the stationary bicycle
and strove with machines in black leather
with names like Double Chest,
Pulldown, Leg Curl, and Leg Extension.
This too failed to bring me happiness.

■

Pete is operating a fishing boat.
He took me out in it once
and we caught a big fish.
Jimmy ascends every morning
in a balloon with colored panels
over Aspen, Colorado.
Jack is "dream-painting." He places a canvas
on his mattress. While he sleeps
it prints the work of the subconscious.

Jane is into Yoga, standing on one leg
with her eyes closed. She opens her eyes,
sighs, and goes into the house.

THE NATURALIST AND THE VOLCANO

Sometimes I climb to the top of the hill
with a book. It is peaceful here
in the circle made by the ruins.

In Roman times, somewhere on the sides
of this promontory "that divides the wind,"
stood two villas. "Comedy" and "Tragedy"
Pliny called them—the Younger Pliny
whose *Letters* I have been reading.
There were two Plinys . . .
Pliny who wrote a *Natural History*
and his nephew who wrote letters.

The older Pliny died in an eruption
of Vesuvius. As his nephew tells it,
the "savant" wanted a closer look . . .
and to come to the help of a friend.
So, being an admiral, he ordered out a ship.

"Ashes and hot stones were falling
and the captain wanted to turn back,
but he said, 'Fortune befriends the brave,
carry me to Pompionanus!' "

On arriving he called for a bath,
then sat down to dinner, talking informally
to set their fears at rest.

And all that night while Vesuvius
was thundering, Pliny slept.
Those who were close to the door
could hear him "breathing heavily
because he was pretty fat."

The day dawned black as pitch
and the house was shaking to the foundations.
So, says the writer, "balancing reasons,"
they decided to make a run for it,
and wrapped napkins around their heads.

But the sea was against them,
so Pliny lay down. There was a smell of sulphur,
he struggled to stand. . . .
Days later his body was found beneath the ashes.

Was this Tragedy? I don't think
that Pliny would have thought so,
being a naturalist, caught up
in the study of his subject,
the volcano . . . "like a pine tree
shooting up to a great height,
the trunk spreading at the top
into branches . . . at one moment white,
at another dark and spotted."

THE FLAUBERT PAVILION

1

"The Flaubert Museum is closed."

"And the house at Croisset?"

"That is open," she conceded."

The bus drove through the streets of Rouen,
then down a hill.
            The *Hirondelle*
used to go rattling down, carrying Emma
to a rendezvous with Leon . . .
and slowly back, with the hideous
blind beggar trudging beside it
singing about a young girl in love.

I had a vision of Croisset.
There would be fields and haystacks,
a smell of apples fermenting,
stone walls, and roofs of thatch.

The bus skirted a harbor
with freighters and tankers tied up,
and a forest of cranes . . . where Felicité
saw horses dangling in mid-air
and thought she was losing her mind.

Suddenly, next to a municipal building,
the bus came to a stop. "Croisset,"
said the driver, and got off.

2

A sign pointed to "The Flaubert Pavilion."
We walked . . . along a row of houses
that faced the road and the Seine.
Then the high wall of a factory . . .
A truck came out, carrying large rolls,
and there were bales of old newspaper
in the factory yard.

We crossed over and walked by the Seine.
There was no sidewalk, only rusting rails.
We tried walking on the ties for a while,
then crossed back again. Finally
we came to the pavilion. It was closed.
From twelve to two, said a sign.

Very well, it would give us time
for lunch. And we were hungry.

3

There was a crossing in the distance
with a traffic light.
Perhaps there would also be shops.

We walked toward it. Cars and trucks went by.
Apparently no one ever stopped
in this road. We were the only people.
The houses seemed uninhabited.

Then we came to a sign . . . "Le Pulque."
The restaurant, for such it was,
had bright yellow, Mexican walls.

A dozen people seated at the tables
were putting the food away—
four courses with wine, forty francs.
We ordered *Quenelles de Brochet.*
The owner came over to see how we'd liked them.
He was a stout, fair man with a moustache,
in his shirt sleeves, *vrai Normand.*

The walls were dedicated to the chase
with hunting horns and shotguns.
I thought of Flaubert sitting there,
eavesdropping.

             "I tell you I see her
sneaking over there through the fields."

"Go on, you're making it up."

"Am I? The other morning, at daybreak
just as I was sighting a bird,

up she popped. I gave her what for!
She could have got herself shot."

4

We rang. A dog barked
and an elderly woman came to the door.
She seemed surprised to have visitors.

The house of Flaubert no longer existed,
she informed us. It stood on ground
now occupied by the paper factory.
The pavilion was all that remained.

We gave her the small entrance fee.
She thanked us, and led the way.

Most of his furniture was in the museum.
There were only a few objects of interest
apportioned here by the State.

Some pages of writing under glass,
the "comice agricole,"
most of the sentences crossed out
and a few words written in . . .

The "working cabinet of Flaubert" . . .
clay pipes, looking frail and pitiful,
a pair of slippers, a bronze Buddha,
and—a real treasure—a parrot

said to have been Felicité's.
A green, ordinary-looking bird . . .
yet it had served as *succedaneum*
of the Spirit, and served Flaubert,
I think, as his final statement:
it is not what a thing is
but what you feel about it that counts.

5

A French friend to whom I told this story,
when I complained about the missing house,
said, "The French are like that.
They have so much, they don't give a damn."

A medical man disagreed.
He said, you can't argue with Progress.

And the need for paper is insatiable.
Hundreds of newspapers and magazines
every day demand their tons.
Reams of paper are needed in offices,
for government, and education.
Without a steady supply of paper
he wouldn't have his medical journals
and I wouldn't have my books.

For industry . . . They even make houses
out of paper in Japan.

All this weighed in the balance with
sentimentality . . . preserving the house
of a writer who, let's face it,
is not to everyone's taste.
A woman, married to a doctor,
commits adultery and runs him into debt. . . .

Society would be none the worse
if Madame Bovary had been recycled.

WHITE OXEN

A man walks beside them
with a whip that he cracks.
The cart they draw is painted
with Saracens and Crusaders,
fierce eyes and ranks of spears.

They are on the steep road
that goes up the mountain.
Their neat-stepping hoofs
appear to be flickering
in the sun, raising dust.

They are higher than the roofs
on which striped gourds and melons
lie ripening. They move
among the dark green olives
that grow on the rocks.

They dwindle as they climb . . .
vanish around a corner
and reappear walking on the edge
of a precipice. They enter
the region of mist and darkness.

I think I can see them still:
a pair of yoked oxen
the color of ivory
or smoke, with red tassels,
in the gathering dusk.

THE BAZUFT

In Persia there's a wandering tribe—
every year they come to a river,

the Bazuft, they all have to cross.
Those who can't are left behind.

The sun warm on the mat, the sound
of the sheep-bell a long way off.

THE RISE

I fished out in the middle
and fished around the shore,
I fished all day and caught nothing . . .
only the creak of oarlocks
and the cry of a moorhen
and beat of geese flying over.

The next day Monaghan came
in his van. Joe's an artist
and one of the best fly fishermen.
I said they ought to stock the lake.
No, he said, for the small fish
take everything. The big ones
grow despondent and lie on the bottom.

That night he took me out with him.
No rowing . . . he had an outboard motor.
We anchored off a point in the dark
and waited.

            Around ten-thirty
the night came alive with splashes.
He stood and cast, lunging toward the sound.
The rise lasted for half an hour
and when the night was still again
he had caught three lovely fish.

Some day I'd like to go back
and hear the cry of a moorhen
and learn from Monaghan how to fish.

A FUSE LINK

Here lie James and Drucilla Gordy;
Zeddock K. Evans, 1812–1863;
Hezekiah Shockley, Arabella Shockley,

and an acre of bad writing:
"Till Thy Name Shall Every Grief Remove
With Life. With Memory. And With Love."

Must love be forgotten?
O God, Horatio, what wounded names
(words standing thus misplaced) shall live behind us!

■

Can it be? Yes, it is . . .
parked by the service station.
We'll kiss and make up,
pretend it never happened.

The mechanic has something to show me
in the palm of his hand:
"This is what did it."
I stare, and he explains, "A fuse link."

A flat little piece of metal
scarcely bigger than an earring.
A fuse link. Of course, that would explain everything.

94

■

Goodbye to the bronze Napoleon,
the cemetery on the hill
and smoke at the heart of a valley.

It's good to be traveling again
though I'm in a single lane
behind an old Studebaker

with children in the back making faces,
holding up their Cabbage Patch dolls,
sticking out their tongues,

for so many miles
I am practically one of the family.

SUMMER COMES TO THE THREE VILLAGES

The people come off the ferry,
cross East Broadway
to Main Street, and go into the stores.

The cars come down the ramp
and drive around, sightseeing.
They admire the white church on the corner.

■

Dick Bone is in his drive
working on his boat, replacing old boards
with new ones, fixing the bilge-pump.

I watch him when I am not writing,
listening to the sounds of birds
and the traffic out on the road.

■

There is the picnic on the Fourth of July
with a softball game, a three-legged race,
and an outdoor barbecue.

Red flares on the road . . . drive slower.
There's glass in the road . . . an ambulance,
a car skewed across the road.

96

■

A friend was dying of throat cancer.
He seized the slate round his neck
and wrote fiercely . . . an indecipherable scrawl.

You could think of nothing to say,
and what could anyone do?
Only this—still be thinking about him.

■

This is the time when calamus has grown
almost to its full height,
lining the water. A green wall.

These are the days when not a leaf stirs
and everyone complains of the humidity,
and the boughs grow dark as the sky whitens.

The smoke of summer rises from the Three Villages
like incense in the sight of God
and he smells it and pronounces it good.

HIS AND HERS

We've a cook named Gaston,
a dishwasher, Manuel,
a gardener, and a chauffeur.

When there's anything to be done
I simply give it to the one
who's responsible. You may think
it's me up here on a ladder,

but it's not—it's the chauffeur
who also doubles as a handyman.
I myself am at Shea Stadium

pinch-hitting for the Mets in the ninth
with two out and two men on.

■

The Smith Haven Mall . . .
nine miles. She could walk from here.

Nicolls Road . . . seven miles.

How about calling a cab?
In my wife's out-of-gas scenario
no one will let her use the phone.
Besides, how do you know?
The householder could be a homicidal maniac.

And the AAA keep asking
for exact directions. What's the name
of the nearest cross street, which she doesn't know.

So she has to walk all the way.

WAITING IN THE SERVICE STATION

Waiting in the service station,
reading *Sports Illustrated,*

listening to every sound
and wondering, is it mine? . . .

When they say the car is ready
and I go to pay the bill

I'm relieved, I'd pay anything
to be out of there, on the road,

moving with the traffic,
looking at the buildings and signs:

Clams 'n Stuff, Scelfo Realty,
Candi's X-Rated Dancers.

IT FIGURES

I've been talking to our cleaning woman.
Her husband's a traffic policeman.
They've opened a shop that sells
automobile tires . . . and another shop
close by, to sell artificial flowers.

She'll make them herself, out of silk
and wire, arranged in a bouquet . . .
for weddings and birthdays,
and "because when a man buys a new tire
he'll want to take flowers home to his wife."

NEIGHBORS

The Boat Restorer

Dick's bought an old boat.
He'll scrape her right down,

caulk, sandpaper, varnish,
and name her "Island Rose."

The Running Woman

They say the court took away her children
and awarded them to the father.
"That's what you get," they say, "for fooling
    around."

I've seen her running on highways, in side
    streets,
along the water and back again,
in all kinds of weather. Sometimes twice a day.

The Cold Man

He is wearing an overcoat
indoors, in the middle of summer,
and all the windows are closed.

His wife comes in carrying a tray . . .
little glasses of cowslip wine
and some cookies. We each take one.

I see him again, in Gristede's.
It's cold . . . the air-conditioning.
"I'm cold," he says, "but they don't care."

A Property Owner

Old man mad about property . . .
thinks because he pays taxes

he owns the beach and the sea.
What's he shouting now? "King's rights!"

Another Property Owner

A man rides up on a bicycle
and dismounts. He is Chinese.

The owner has sent him to tell us
to leave. "He very mean."

The property is under surveillance.
The owner sits watching a screen.

The shadows of the wood are long,
a sparrow hops onto the lawn.

Darby and Joan

"Six years she lived with Rosenstein.
I figured it out . . .
I told her, '936 times
at least, you were laid by a dwarf.' "

The object of this arithmetic,
an old woman with white hair,
sits by herself in the kitchen
eating yoghurt and a banana.

The Poet

Sounds of traffic on 25A,
a plane slowly circling . . .

as though a world were building
its likeness through the ear.

A BRAMBLE BUSH

One night in winter Willa went missing.
I took my Irish raincoat, gloves,
and a flashlight.

    In half an hour
I had her and the wood had me,
caught in brambles. I couldn't use my hands—
if I set her down she'd run off again.

So I stood there, seeing the irony,
lights only a hundred yards away,
and hearing sounds of television:
the murmur of a voice, or voices,
followed by a roar of applause . . .
some situation comedy or stand-up comedian.

    ■

Winter has passed, and it is spring again
when the small green buds with forked tails
like fishes swim on the wind.
Then summer, gold on green . . .
Looking at the sky through the leaves
is like looking through shining crystal.

Then the leaves come drifting down,
and it's December. Frau Holle

fills the sky with white feathers.
Rain falls and freezes. The boughs are sheathed
in ice, with bright icicles hanging down
like lace. The whole wood glitters.

■

After some prolonged litigation
between the Town and the man who owns the land
the wood stands on, it has been agreed
to cut the trees down and build houses.
The development is to be called Birchwood
and zoned for half or quarter acres.

And so, one spring, comes the surveyor
squinting through his telescope. "Joe,"
he shouts, "look behind you!
What's that in the bush?"

                              Joe looks and sees,
tangled in thorns, the skeleton of a man
still holding the skeleton of a dog.

■

A cold gust of air set the wood rustling.
Lightning flashed. There was a roll of thunder.
But this was not my kind of story.
I turned around with my back to the brambles
and, holding the dog to my chest,
hurled myself backward.

They gave a little. I did it again . . .
and so, standing and falling, made lunatic progress
until I fell out of a bush into the open.

I rested a while, then put her on the leash,
and walked the short way home, arriving
as the first cold raindrops fell.

SEA OF GRASS

For Jimmy Ernst

If you're a Jew and want to know
which transport your mother was on,
the French railroads have a list.
Jimmy showed me the name of his:
"Lou Straus-Ernst . . . Transport 76."

One of those who made the journey
and survived, gave an account:
"Seventy would be put in a boxcar.
There would be a long wait
while the train was boarded up.
Then three days' travel east . . .
paper mattresses on the floor
for the sick, bare boards for the rest.
Many did not survive."

■

At Auschwitz shortly before the end
one had seen her: "A woman totally exhausted,
half lying, half leaning against a wall,
warming herself in the last rays of a dying sun."

And still we believe in loving-kindness . . .
some even believe there's a God.
This is a mystery, *ein Rätsel*
God himself could not explain.

■

A few minutes' walk from the house
where I live, there's a beach,
a brown strip of sand
lined with tide-wrack and litter . . .
boards, plastic bottles
and, at the water's edge, green reeds.

"Sea of Grass" Jimmy called it.
Every time I come here I think of him
and his painting.

"Work!
God wants you to," said Flaubert.

There they are every summer
just as he painted them,
growing up again . . . a hedge
of stems and leaves standing motionless.

Blue water, and a harbor's mouth
opening into the sky.

ON A PAINTING BY JIMMY ERNST

A line of masked dancers
facing you, their eyes are slits . . .
holding rattles in their hands,
the sky behind them on fire . . .
Max Ernst and Paul Eluard,
Giacometti, Man Ray, Miró,
Soupault . . . all the Surrealists
lighting up the sky of Paris . . .
all the Kachina Indians!

TROUBLE

I went to see my old friend
Greg.

He was in the kitchen
slicing radishes.

I explained
what had brought me. He said,
"Let me see if I understand.
You're worried because you're happy?"

I said, "It's not so absurd.
Take any writer, even Tolstoy . . .
he talks about happy families
being all the same. Misery,
that's all people care about.
They won't go to a concert
unless it's discordant, a ballet
unless it takes place in a hospital
and the dancers are wound in bandages."

"Enough," he said, "already.
What do you care about such people?"

Having made the salad, he decided
it was his to do with as he pleased . . .
put his fingers in and mucked it about,
picked out a mushroom.
"Stay for dinner," he said. I said no thanks.

■

I take my trouble to bed with me.
When I wake in the morning
it's there, refreshed by a good night's sleep.

Writing poetry used to be easy.
"The stag at eve had drunk his fill"
got you off to a running start.

"What are you thinking?"
says Miriam, who for some time
has been awake.

                    "I ought to do something
post-structural. A monkey version
of *Hamlet.*"

She says, "I don't follow."

"It's a theory. If you chain monkeys
to typewriters, one of them
sooner or later will write *Hamlet.*
I'll write it, changing a few words . . ."

"Shakespeare," she says.
"Shakespeare was the monkey,

the one who typed *Hamlet*
exactly, word for word."

I stare at her, stunned
and speechless with admiration.

■

I'm looking out the window
at a beagle, a beagle-terrier,
and a westie. Some trees.
A sky empty and void of ideas.

I think the powers that be
have decided, "That's enough,
no more poetry for this fellow,
just life, since he likes it so much.

From where we sit, on Olympus,
as far as we can see
it's dirt and weeds and bricks
with creatures crawling between.

What we like is a burnt offering . . .
not just cooked, scorched black,
a heart turning on a spit
over the fires of greed
and lust and self-loathing.

But a white birch by a door,
sunlight breaking from a cloud,

yellow and purple tips
pushing up from the ground,
and the woman he's so fond of . . .

if that's all he wants, let him have it,
there's nothing we can do for him."

VILLA

SELENE

VILLA SELENE

June 16, 1988

My mother lives at Viareggio in Italy. Five weeks ago she fell and broke a thighbone. She was operated on and is recovering.

Yesterday Miriam and I flew to Italy, traveling by Alitalia. The flight was delayed at Kennedy Airport for an hour and a half. When we arrived in Rome we ran to catch the connecting flight to Pisa. We arrived at the gate to find that the plane had just left and there would not be another flight to Pisa for six and a half hours.

A man at the Alitalia counter assured us that a "telex" would be sent to Pisa saying we were booked on the next flight. And Alitalia would provide lunch for the stranded passengers. The lunch consisted of the cheapest items on the menu and proved to be inedible. We hung around the airport all afternoon. In running to make the connection I had lost my glasses—they must have fallen from a pocket. They were new and I had scarcely used them.

The flight to Pisa took thirty-five minutes. We were met by Renato Barsanti, my mother's husband. He had also met the earlier flight and telephoned Rome to find out why we were not on it—Alitalia had not sent the "telex." Renato had a taxi waiting. As Miriam had never seen the Leaning Tower he told the driver to take the road that went by it. It was the rush hour, around six p.m., and the traffic was heavy. It seems that every family in Italy now owns a car.

We drove for forty minutes on a road lined with trees, passing houses with yellow walls and fields under cultivation. The country is flat with a view of mountains. Dante speaks of them—he says that these are the mountains that prevent the Pisans from seeing Lucca.

Rosalind and Renato live on the long street in Viareggio that runs parallel to the sea, changing its name as it goes. We went upstairs right away to see my mother. She was sitting up in a chair. We were shocked at her appearance. She is ninety-two or -three. Up to now she has been able to take twenty years off her age, but now she is in pain and looks very old. She is aware of everything going on around her, but is distracted by the pain and finds it hard to follow a conversation.

She wishes to be in New York . . . "to die" she tells Grazia, the woman who lives downstairs and works as housekeeper, cook, and nurse. But this is an impossible wish. In Viareggio Rosalind has nurses around the clock, one arriving as another leaves, and the doctor makes a house call every day. Try finding that kind of care in New York! The last time Rosalind and Renato were in New York they hired a woman from some South American country who made off with as much of Rosalind's jewelry as she could lay her hands on.

For dinner on our first evening in Viareggio, Renato took us to Ristorante Tito del Molo, at the far end of the street. Tito's has a wonderful menu—we began with a seafood antipasto. The service at Tito's is also wonderful—Renato's friend, l'Avvocato (the Lawyer), calls it "the choreography." But Miriam and I were too tired. This was a pity, for Tito's is also extremely expensive.

6/17

Grazia made breakfast for us, but we shall be taking our other meals out—Grazia has her hands full. As she says, the villa is like a clinic.

Miriam and I went walking on Viale Carducci, as the street is called at this point. The side on which the villa stands, facing the sea, has residences and hotels. There is a median strip with palm trees. The side next the sea is lined with eating places, bathing establishments, and shops. Some of the names have changed since I was here last—there is now a Mondo Disco. But the street, says Renato, never changes.

Later in the morning we sat and talked with Rosalind. Besides the pain in her legs she is tormented by a burning and itching of the skin.

Renato took us to a restaurant, Montecatini, for lunch, and left us there. He brought us back to the same restaurant for dinner. We are to charge our meals to the Barsanti account. The food at Montecatini is very good, especially the antipasto table with twenty dishes, mostly seafood, to choose from, and the prices are not nearly as high as at Tito's.

We walked back to the villa, about two kilometers. The Italians had just won a football match against Denmark and cars raced down the street blowing their horns, with the flag flying.

6/18

Heavy rain and thunder during the night. This morning sat with Rosalind while she talked, reminiscing about her life on East Broadway more than seventy years ago. The family lived on the lower floor. When someone brought her home she said she lived on the second floor because it had a doctor's office and was more prestigious.

She talked about Jamaica. When she went back years later Douglas Fletcher wanted her to see her old house, Volyn, and she went and looked around. It was upsetting to see the furniture of the people who lived there now. She remembered the name of my headmaster, Mr. Fraser . . . he wrote her saying that I would be a "star." Talked about her first job in New York, cutting threads on blouses with tucks—how difficult this was . . . she made holes in the material. Was paid $4 a week—.75¢ a day.

She traveled to Jamaica as one of Annette Kellerman's bathing beauties to make a movie. Annette Kellerman was twenty-five and had a "special relationship" with the director, and was jealous of any young, pretty woman. Rosalind was a poor swimmer, so a friend, one of the girls whose father worked as a technician, making statues for the movie, swam beside her and saw that she didn't sink.

Reminiscing about her life as a saleslady traveling in cosmetics . . . She was on the road in the United States for two years, then in South and Central America. Was in a hurricane in Mexico, on a high floor, the building shaking and the lights out. In San Salvador during a revolution . . . the city burning. The next day a young man asked if she wanted to go for a drive. She said yes. He drove to the hospital to see his friend who had been hurt the day before. She saw weapons on the floor of the car, and he said that people were trying to kill him for his actions of the day before. He had brought her along as insurance! She told him to take her back right away.

Rubinstein paid her $50 a month and another $50 for expenses. She arranged matters so that she could come to Jamaica and see her children, on the supposition—which was unfounded—that she could do business there. It is terrible to be doing work you don't like and not see a way out.

We heard once more how she took the Clipper to New York against Madame's wishes and presented her with the idea of having a branch of the company in Venezuela. In Caracas she bought an old house. Things didn't go well until a tree in front of the house was cut down and she added a level to the building and a sign, "Helena Rubinstein." People thought that she was Helena Rubinstein. A colonel, a friend of hers, had the tree removed in the night by two convicts, otherwise it might have been impossible—trees were protected by the state.

Grazia made lunch for us today: pasta with a meat sauce, roast chicken, green peas, cheese, fruit, and coffee (espresso). Cooked by Grazia, served by Grazia and the cleaning woman, Giovanna.

More conversation with Rosalind, including one of her monologues about the money she has in banks . . . in Monaco, in Caracas and, now she adds, in Lucca. When the time comes I am to go to these countries and collect the money she has left in my name. But she does not say what banks. I imagine myself in Monaco, Venezuela, Italy, going from bank to bank and speaking to officials who, shrugging their shoulders, deny the existence of any such account.

After this session, however, she gives me an old address book to copy from . . . it has addresses of her banks in Monaco and Lucca. She has always been careful not to part with this kind of information—it is not a good sign that she is willing to do so now. I'd rather not talk about money, but if we are to talk let it be to the point, not these vague instructions. But she finds it hard to come to the point. The money is what she has to show for her years of hard work. It's not just money, it's her life.

She is continually in pain. There is the broken femur—a plate has been inserted. There is a "hole" or opening in her back that has to heal. There is the itching of the skin, *prurito.* In order for her to urinate they have inserted a catheter, which is very painful. And this is not all: for years she has suffered from arthritis. And this morning upon waking she felt as if she were being suffocated by a weight pressing down. Miriam suggests that she has been too heavily medicated so that she can sleep and that they should reduce the medication.

In the evening Miriam and I eat at Tito's. I ask to see the bill though it's being charged to Barsanti. The waiter brings a strip from the cash register with a column of figures. I have an impression that they add up to $200. Can this be possible? I should look at the figures closely but my mind goes blank.

6/19

Renato has rented a car for us, a small Fiat. He says that more of these cars are sold than any other car in the world. Miriam and I drive to Pisa where we look at the cathedral, the Leaning Tower, and the Campo Santo. I want her to see the murals by the master of "The Triumph of Death." The "Inferno" with its bull head of Satan made a strong impression on me when I first saw it thirty years ago. We lunch at a restaurant with tables outdoors and a view of the tower with people walking around it. I once climbed up there but wouldn't try it now. I have dreams about falling—the Leaning Tower is a waking nightmare.

In the evening, at Viareggio, we walk to the Ristorante Montecatini and back. It is Sunday with lots of young people strolling and hanging out. A feeling of friendliness and young love in the air . . . a moon like the peg of an orange. If you're young the place to be is Italy . . . not bad for the old ones either.

Reading Richard Burgin's *Conversations with Isaac Bashevis Singer . . .* I agree with Singer about many things, this for example:

> It's only the amateur who will take any topic. He will go somewhere, he will hear a story—something, anything—and immediately it will become "his story." The real writer writes only stories which are connected with his personality, with his character, with his way of seeing the world.

But Singer has narrow views. On verse . . . people no longer read it because poets have abandoned narrative and rhyme. This is like the conversation I had with him years ago in Fort Worth. He came to my reading and liked it, but asked why I didn't rhyme. He says here that Homer is the greatest poet. When did Homer rhyme?

6/20

Miriam's advice about lowering the medication has worked wonders. This morning Rosalind woke without the feeling of weight and suffocation.

She talked for a long time . . . about purchasing the villa for the Engineer, Renato's brother Benvenuto who died a few years ago. She told Benvenuto, "A man in your position should have a residence worthy of him," and persuaded him to buy the Villa Selene, facing the beach property that belonged to the Barsantis. The villa had been allowed to deteriorate, but when she saw the marble staircase she knew that Benvenuto ought to buy it. She undertook the renovation . . . everything had to be done over, the plumbing, electricity, everything. She sent one of the carpets to an abbey to be mended.

Rosalind doesn't engage in conversation, she delivers a monologue. Afterwards Miriam tells me that she understands how I have been able to get along with my mother over the years . . . by ignoring her.

Once more . . . the story about Rosalind and Renato's trip to Israel. They saw a poor immigrant carrying a cheap suitcase made of straw. He had a dignified appearance in spite of his poverty. Rosalind sent Renato over to ask him, "Is there anything we can do for you?" The man said, "No thanks, I don't want anything." Imagine that! A poor man who refused to accept money!

In the afternoon Miriam and I sit on the beach at Antaura, part of the Barsanti holdings. We're received like royalty, given a cabin to change in, a beach umbrella, and deck chairs. But the water is too cold for swimming.

The sea is gray-green. There are rows of beach umbrellas . . . blue, green, blue with horizontal red stripes, etc., each with two chairs. The sand is brown.

There's a young couple next to us, the woman with a heavy growth of hair under her arms . . . un-American. I talk to the young man and he says that his father is a friend of Renato and Renato's brother, Giorgio. Italy is just one big family.

I am reading Seamus Heaney's poems in order to write the article promised to a man in Ireland. I begin at the beginning, with *Poems 1965–1975.*

A black man walks by with a case of sunglasses, watches, and purses. We decline to buy. The black men on the beach at Viareggio are very black . . . like the Africans you used to see in children's books.

I have an idea for the article that may not work out . . . an outsider's, that is, non-Irishman's view. I would examine Heaney's poetry to see if it can be detached from references to a particular culture. Is there "pure poetry"? Such thinking would be opposed to Williams's theory of "locality." I may decide, after all, that poetry is always "married to earth," as Williams, John Dewey, and Keyserling thought.

We plan to have lunch at Lidino, the bathing establishment next to Antaura. Grazia comes down to the beach to tell us to charge the meal to Barsanti. It's a good lunch: a platter of fried fish, mixed—shrimp, eel, calamari, etc.—with French fries, a lettuce salad, and wine. The waiter brings effervescent white wine instead of the "non frizzante" we ordered, but we drink it anyway. I mention the mistake to the waitress, and the waiter turns up with two bottles of noneffervescent wine for us to choose from. We have to persuade him that we don't need them now. Miriam has ice cream and we both have espressos. The waiter puts Miriam's coffee into her ice cream and this is very good.

I keep thinking about the murals in the Campo Santo. They were painted in the late fourteenth century, at the time of the Black Death. "The Triumph of Death" is a warning, with envy and malice behind it, to the people who are having a good time, listening to music, riding palfreys, and so on. There are three open coffins with putrefying bodies over which snakes or worms are crawling. Some ladies on horseback are looking into the coffins and one is holding her nose.

In the "Universal Judgement" there are some nasty surprises on the faces of the kings, nobles, and priests who are being rejected and sent to Hell. The "Inferno," as I've said, is my favorite. The damned are being pushed or dragged to the mouth of a dragon, with demons gnawing on them as they go. On the hide of the "bovine Satan" are what look like suction cups—they appear to have been derived from the octopus. After these scenes living in a cave in North Africa comes as a relief—it's possible to avoid Hell if you live like a hermit. See how

126

abjectly the two demons make off when the holy father rejects their temptations of wine, women, and song!

Over lunch Miriam and I discuss the difference between a hallucination and an apparition. The ghost in *Hamlet* is an apparition—it is seen by several people. A hallucination is subjective. I tell Miriam that she was an apparition.

It was in Darien, Connecticut. I had given a poetry reading and was trying to sign books with one hand and hold a glass of wine in the other. A voice said, "I'll hold that for you," and a hand took the glass. Then I couldn't find the top of my pen and was clapping a hand to my pockets. The voice said, "There's one you haven't tried yet." I turned, and the hand pointed to my breast pocket. The pen top was in it. I looked at the owner of the hand and voice—she wasn't only gifted with second sight, she was beautiful.

For Outstanding Merit

There were six Barsanti brothers. The family owned extensive property in Viareggio. During the war it was confiscated by Mussolini. They got it back after the war, but now they were poor—their only income came from Giorgio's playing football. He was an international football star and contributed from his earnings to the support of his mother and brothers.

Renato Barsanti was tall, good-looking, and a snappy dresser. He escorted the most beautiful ladies and dined in the best restaurants. Everybody liked Renato. His old-

127

est brother, Benvenuto, was short and ugly—no woman would look at him twice. But Benvenuto was good at his studies; he studied hard and became an engineer.

Benvenuto and Renato went to South America to seek their fortune. They started in the Argentine where Benvenuto imported Italian labor and built roads and airports. Renato went to Venezuela and wired Benvenuto to come—the country was undeveloped and offered unheard-of opportunities.

Benvenuto made a fortune in the engineering business. He had a fleet of machines in Italy as well as South America. Renato found a job with a beer company, but they didn't like him because he wouldn't put a pencil in his shirt pocket and comport himself like a clerk.

Renato applied for a position with Helena Rubinstein in Caracas. It was so that he met Rosalind de Marantz who owned the business.

The Engineer had a principle: no one should marry. He held a grudge against Renato for marrying Rosalind. Not that he didn't like her . . . he did, in so far as it lay in him to like anyone. And Rosalind had her own money.

When Rosalind retired from business she and Renato moved to Italy. They bought a villa at San Alessio, near Lucca, and named it Villa Rosalinda. In the years that followed Benvenuto would give Renato jobs to do for him in the Rome office of the company, and sometimes he asked Renato to come to Venezuela to help him in the business there. Renato was happy to oblige—besides, a man should have some work to do.

When Benvenuto died he was worth thirty million dollars. He left Renato the income on a million, $10,000 a month, for life. But Renato couldn't touch the principal. The rest of the estate, a huge fortune, was left to Giorgio, Renato's younger brother who had not exerted himself for years, not since kicking a football and hitting it with his head.

Giorgio has no wife and, as far as is known, no children. He lives in Miami and comes to Viareggio from time to time, when he stays at one of the beach houses that are part of the estate. The house was once renovated with American appliances. When Giorgio arrived and saw this he had the plumbing and appliances ripped out and thrown in the street. The kitchen had been newly wallpapered. Giorgio bought some cans of paint and painted it red, white, and blue. No one can explain why he did this.

Renato owns a fourth part of Villa Selene. Giorgio cannot evict Renato and Rosalind, for they have lived there for fifteen years and the law says that if you have lived in a place for that length of time you cannot be evicted. But he would evict them if he could.

Renato feels badly used, after all the work he did for the company. But he is a lot better off than Fortunato, who was Benvenuto's chauffeur and companion. Fortunato was more than an employee, assisting Benvenuto from the moment he got up in the morning until he went to bed at night. Fortunato lived like a gentleman; as Benvenuto's companion he was accustomed to "moving in the world," eating in restaurants and staying at hotels. But Benvenuto in his will left his employees nothing— not a thousand lire note to show for their years of service.

And Fortunato was out of a job. He drives a taxi now

and feels rather bitter—he is a married man with three children.

In Viareggio, Benvenuto is regarded as a public benefactor for his contributions to charity. Renato had the idea and made the arrangements . . . giving the Commune an ambulance and three dialysis machines.

The Italian government made Benvenuto a Knight of Labor, and when he died he was buried in Viareggio with an elaborate ceremony. A certificate on the wall at Villa Selene reads as follows:

Ai Lucchesi Che Hanno
Onorato L'Italia Nel
Mondo

Camera di Commercio LUCCA
Industria Artigianato Agricoltura

Diploma di Benemerenza
conferito a Barsanti Benvenuto
"alla memoria"

nato a Viareggio il
22–2–1903   12–10–1985

7 Set 1986

Il Presidente

Franco Fratellini

The diploma has a floret with two tails hanging down and a seal in the shape of a shield. There is a circle of writing around the seal, but the ink is blurred and the words cannot be made out.

6/21

This morning we drove to Lucca. The *autostrade* takes some getting used to. Cars go by at high speed, paying no attention to the posted limit.

In Lucca we walked about the narrow streets, especially Via Fillungo, looking in the shop windows. I know Lucca well . . . used to come here often from the Villa Rosalinda, a few kilometers away.

We had lunch in an area overlooked by apartment windows with laundry hanging out, then coffee in the Piazza dei Mercanti. We went to St. Martin's to see Ilaria, the lady with the pet dog lying at her feet and looking up at her. Miriam said that our dogs don't lie like that with their hind legs drawn up, but when we got back to Viareggio we saw that this is how Tico, the dog at the villa, lies down.

Rosalind seems stronger. We had a conversation about her life in Jamaica. She doesn't recall how many years she lived there—she said five, but I pointed out that it must have been at least twelve. She married my father in 1916 and came to Jamaica in '17. She left in 1930 and went to Toronto where she sold Elizabeth Arden cosmetics, because some Canadian tourists in Kingston said they'd sponsor her.

This conversation was precipitated by my saying that when we were in Lucca I decided against our paying a visit to the Villa Rosalinda—I didn't believe in reliving the past. Rosalind said that once she had left the villa she never went back.

I am sitting on the balcony with Miriam. It's seven forty-five and the sun is still shining. We look across the bathhouses and beach . . . across Lidino, Antaura, Principe, Petrini, Lita, and Tirista. The sea is gray-blue and a freighter has been anchored on the horizon for days. A ship waiting to sail makes you think of leaving for distant places, for sights and sounds you can't imagine.

> My child, my sister, dream
> How sweet all things would seem
> Were we in that kind land to live together . . .

But really, people are impossible! Here I'm living in a villa in Italy, and it's not enough, I'm thinking of somewhere else and bovarizing. It's as Baudelaire said: "Life is a hospital where every patient is obsessed by the desire of changing beds." Where, he asks his soul, would you like to go? To Lisbon where it's warm? Rotterdam with its ships moored on doorsteps? Batavia, where "the wit of Europe" is "wedded to the beauty of the tropics?" Shall it be the Baltic? The Pole where the Aurora Borealis shoots up its rose-red sheafs like reflections of the fireworks of hell?

"At last my soul explodes! 'Anywhere! Just so it is out of the world!' "

I have been reading *Curtain: Poirot's Last Case.* Agatha

Christie is not the kind of mystery writer who creates a meticulously plotted and timed puzzle. Christie writes about "characters." But her characters are clichés: the hearty colonel, shy bird-watcher, invalid wife, man-hungry nurse, brusque scientist, fiercely independent young woman. But though she deals in stereotypes the dialogue is frequently stiff and out of character. This doesn't do her any harm with the public who think in stereotypes and so don't think at all.

I don't envy popular writers their success. I write for pleasure, not for a living, and the pleasure comes of having an idea no one seems to have had or to have expressed in the same way. To write like Agatha Christie is not to have a life of one's own but to be always trying to please. You're at the beck and call of the public and have to provide the clichés it wants to hear.

6/22

Rosalind seems much better this morning—she's had a tub bath for the first time since her fall.

She talked about her life in Toronto. She lived at the Royal York Hotel, but being a single woman had its drawbacks. You weren't allowed to have guests—on every floor there was a man sitting at a desk who watched as you went to your room.

About her work at Helena Rubinstein's. . . People were envious of her success and the higher salary she was getting, but Madame told Mr. Augenblick, "Leave that woman alone!"

A sign of her feeling better is that she is able to pay attention to others. She questioned Miriam about her background. We discussed the behavior of children . . . their unwillingness to write a letter. I said that it was due to the disorder of my private life, divorce and so on. My mother agreed . . . too promptly, I thought. Miriam said no, it was due to their nature at birth.

Rosalind gave us L500,000 as an anniversary present—tomorrow is our third wedding anniversary. She also said that we may have the still life by Braque. This will take some arranging, however. We'll need a letter from her stating that it's a gift—I anticipate all sorts of trouble with the Customs. We'd better have Renato's lawyer draw up a document.

On the beach . . . a procession of black men with articles to sell: watches, sunglasses, cheap jewelry. Some of them are persistent and stand there after you've said no.

I'm looking over Heaney's poems. I remember clearly his poems about the peat-bog people. I discovered the subject about the same time he did, by reading Glob's book. I was staying at Robert Bly's farm in Minnesota. One night he showed me the book and I took it to bed with me in the converted chicken house. The photographs of bodies found in peat bogs were ghastly and riveting. I wrote a poem about them. Heaney has written several better poems on the same subject. Obviously the Grauballe Man and strangled adultress mean more to him . . . they evoke today's Ireland, the murdered shopkeeper and the woman with her head shaved for going with a soldier. As the subject is more real to him, touching him personally, he has more ideas and creates more images.

He writes about life on the farm, about whins, water-weed, and moss . . . about a cow in calf, eels crossing a field, and barley growing out of dead men's pockets.

It's strange to be reading about such things on a beach in Italy, with a view of brown sand, blue sky, beach umbrellas and deck chairs. A few yards away the restaurant serves *fritto misto:* shrimps, calamari, eel, whiting, sole, mussels, clams, crayfish, dried cod, and smelts.

But Italians also have work to do. Many of these people who look well fed come from poor families . . . and during the war, my God!

Shall we say that at certain times some people are lucky, and others out of luck? And that luck changes . . . that it's turn and turn about, and there's no right or wrong way to live, just luck?

I feel I should say something about life . . . but what? About people lying around in deck chairs, and about the poor. Can it be that those who say that money is everything—in Russia they have another word for it—are right? I shall never believe this—it's not true to my experience. There were days when I couldn't buy a can of beans, yet that didn't seem important—I was thinking about other things.

If the cause of Ireland's suffering is politics, it can be fixed. Or else it can't be fixed. Either way, there is more to life than politics . . . the feeling I have when I read something that matters. This feeling, that I can never describe, is the object of life, the reason we are born, live, and die. And it's the same whether you are in Ireland or Italy.

A woman goes by laden with beach paraphernalia, trailing two small children.

2:15 p.m. The black men who walk the beach with things to sell are taking a siesta. Two of them are lying under the wooden deck of the restaurant, on their sides in the shade.

Over lunch Miriam tells me that when she was a child her brothers, who were in the army, brought home G. I. chocolate, the kind that turned white. She was hungry—her mother was a terrible cook—and she ate it. This was the chocolate we wouldn't eat at the front even when there was nothing else.

After lunch I go for a swim. The water is cold but calm. The last time I swam at Viareggio there was a heavy surf and I went plunging in. There was a strong current like an arm that was trying to carry you away. To my left an Italian boy called "Aiuto!" I shouted to the shore and the lifeguards came out on pontoons propelled by oars, hauled the boy out, and took him to shore.

Then I saw my son Tony coming toward me through the waves. I shouted to him to stop but he kept coming on. I swam to him and told him to turn back, but he was a poor swimmer and unable to make headway against the current. I shouted again for help, and the lifeguards came out and put him on their pontoon boat. When I came to shore there was a circle around him and a woman was scolding him in Italian for endangering his life.

There was nothing I could have done in that current

136

to save him from drowning. I should add that Tony was quite unaware of the danger—he thought he was swimming pretty well.

I felt ashamed. When you are at the mercy of a power much stronger than yourself you don't feel you are being treated unjustly, you aren't filled with rage, you feel ashamed. It's shameful to be weak. Think how ashamed Jews must have felt when the Germans put them in boxcars and sent them off to be gassed. Some may even have felt they deserved it.

Before dinner we had another talk with Rosalind. She wanted to know why all those people in the Michigan book had written about my work. I said, "I'm a good writer." She said that she had liked my early poems but that I had changed "radically." She didn't see the point of writing about someone's painting her toenails—I think she was referring to the poem in which I had a woman shaving her legs. I said that she thought writing should be "beautiful" and take you away from reality, but I believed the opposite: as in a Chekhov story it should show the poetry in common things. She listened to this without understanding. Afterwards Miriam was angry— she said that she restrained herself from saying, "Do you have any idea that your son is an important American poet?"

Rosalind complained about her ailments, and complained about Renato's being from her side—he was downstairs talking to some of his friends. In New York she had him always beside her, but here he sat by her bed only one or two hours a day. He had business to transact with his brother, but what was that to her? She wished she had someone at her side all the time, the way it used to be in families. She quoted some woman who had said that she wished to die quickly with someone holding her hand. One of her sisters who lived in Washington, Ida, had been alone when she died.

We listened to this in silence. She was being very unfair to Renato, who has been devoted and self-sacrificing. In New York he couldn't speak the language and had no friends, but he did the shopping and learned to cook—Renato who always ate in restaurants! When Rosalind had a fall he went to the hospital every day and sat beside her.

She speaks of him as having a good heart and simple, outgoing nature. Renato has more than that—his ideas are always interesting; he has experienced a good deal and thought for himself. He was never able to study like his brother, the Engineer, as he himself is the first to admit, but there is no comparison between Renato and his brothers, the ones I have met. He is worth more than all of them put together.

This evening there was a football match in which Russia defeated Italy. We heard a group of young Italians in the street shouting "Mosca! Mosca!" When the match was over one or two cars went down the street blowing their horns.

I asked Renato why. He said that Italians were good sports and appreciated football even when they lost. But it is one thing to be a good loser, another to cheer for the opposing team. I had a different idea, one that was confirmed some days later by l'Avvocato and his wife over lunch. They said that these young Italians were Communist supporters of the Soviet Union.

6/23

This was the third anniversary of our marriage. We drove to Florence on the *autostrade.* I had visions, as Italians drove past at a hundred miles an hour, of our marriage ending on the anniversary, in a ditch.

It was difficult driving into Florence. I had forgotten how big it is—for some reason I thought of the city as compact, perhaps because I usually came by bus and walked around in the center. But driving to the center was a matter of luck. The traffic was heavy and there were detours and one-way streets to circumvent. It was impossible to find a parking space, but happily we came upon a garage that would take the car for L2000 an hour.

We were looking for a coffee table with a marble top—this was to be our anniversary gift to ourselves. In the Balatresi Gift Shop on the Arno the owner looked up addresses in the phone book and gave us two or three. One was only a few streets away. When I thanked him he said that we were strangers in Florence and he was glad to help. We walked to the place of a marble worker he'd recommended. He was just as helpful, though in a different way. He could make the table for us—he noted the dimensions with a pencil on a block of marble. On the other hand we might be able to find one at . . . and he gave us some addresses, one of them at Pietrasanta, near Viareggio.

Then we crossed a bridge and climbed the hill to San Miniato. The proportions, the roof decorations, the marble carvings, are superb—I think this is the most beautiful building I know.

It's hard to believe, but people have scratched their names on some of the murals. What kind of people are these? Where do they come from, and what can they be thinking?

We had lunch by the river, then went over to the Uffizi. Miriam doesn't care for the Botticellis. She suggests that the reason I like them is that I like the women in the paintings. I'm careful not to respond; it wouldn't help to say that I prefer her to all other women, of any type. She thinks that at any moment I may have a change of heart and even a woman in a painting could be a rival. This is the price one pays for having a bad history as far as women are concerned.

Seen in a street in Florence . . . three men in their twenties dressed as women, with high heels, stockings, brassieres, and earrings. They went into a bar on the corner. People were stopping and making remarks in Italian. Miriam said they looked like unattractive whores.

In the Piazza Signoria they are digging up a buried city. You can see entire rooms that have already been exposed. In the excavation people are carefully brushing the earth away from the stones. They look like foreign students; they probably applied for the work and are doing it for no pay.

There was a lively controversy—some people didn't want the piazza, the heart of Florence, disturbed. But it's

evident that there's another city underlying the one peo-
ple have known for hundreds of years . . . one that was
here before the Medicis and before the Romans.

If you kept on digging in Florence would you keep
discovering buried cities? Where would it stop?

6/24

She was complaining again this morning . . . the old story,
she would rather be in New York. But there's nobody
there she knows, outside Miriam, myself, and her sister
Molly who has an invalid husband to care for.

I said that she was fortunate to be in Viareggio and to
have Renato. But she doesn't want to hear this. She is
suffering to be sure, especially with *prurito,* the burning
of her skin. She complains that her skin feels powdery
when she touches it, like dust.

There followed a scene from a play. The daughter of
a friend of Renato's came to the villa with her child, a
little girl of four, to pay her respects. The woman was
pretty and intelligent, and when she told us she was a
schoolteacher and taught English, Miriam and I were
happy to talk to her . . . a living face in this mausoleum!

Rosalind grew fretful. She said that the child was
bored . . . it was wrong of people not to consider how
easily children were bored. I remarked that the child
wasn't bored, *she* was—and, in fact, the little girl seemed
quite content to be sitting with her mother till the visit
was over. But Rosalind ended by sending mother and
child away. The trouble was that we weren't talking

about her—the only topic, it seems, that can hold her interest.

It is necessary to remind oneself that she is suffering. She has to be helped with the simplest bodily functions. Apart from the pain and discomfort, what humiliation! But when she finds fault with the people who are trying to help her, grumbling at the nurse, at Grazia, it is possible to forget that she is suffering. I find myself thinking that she is selfish and has always been. Not that she is aware of it . . . on the contrary. Everything she has done—moving from one place to another, running a business, deciding to live in Italy—has been for the sake of others.

I think that the belief in Heaven and Hell came from watching old people. If you had peace of mind you left the world easily, angels wafting the soul to Paradise, as in "The Triumph of Death." If you still clung to worldly things—and Rosalind recalls, to the hundred, how much she paid for a gold chain years ago—you were tormented by devils. *Prurito* is one devil, arthritis another. And the more you cling to the world the more devils there are.

Then I remember that she is suffering. And in the copy of *The Dhammapada* I left here on a previous visit, telling my mother she might want to read it, I come across this saying: "Think not of the faults of others, of what they have done or not done. Think rather of your own sins, of the things you have done or not done."

Miriam is distressed by Rosalind's telling the mother and child to leave, and by the growing dislike she feels. This is what really troubles her—she doesn't want to dislike the person in whose house she is staying. It is all the more troubling because she has liked, even loved, Rosalind up to now.

I tell her that the feeling of revulsion is natural and she shouldn't blame herself. But it may help to think of Rosalind's behavior, her wanting everyone to pay attention to her needs, her desires, to the exclusion of everything else, as another illness, like *prurito.*

6/25

Vincenza, one of Rosalind's nurses, knows a place in Pietrasanta that may be able to make our coffee table, and she goes with us so we won't be charged fancy tourist prices. The owner is a friend of hers.

Blocks of marble are being sawn and the air is filled with a soft white dust like face powder. The marble comes from Portugal and Turkey as well as Carrara, and in several colors, white and green and rose. We decide on white Carrara with gray swirls. The table will be shipped to New York and should arrive in six weeks.

We drive back for lunch at Torre del Lago with Renato, l'Avvocato, and the Avvocato's wife and daughter. Elisabetta is a sixteen-year-old schoolgirl, dark, pretty, and tall—too tall to be the ballerina she wanted to be. She had to choose between ballet school and a regular school that awards a teaching license—she chose to study for the license. She has been to England to learn English but cannot speak it at all.

Her mother is dark, bright-eyed, and vivacious. She wears layers of makeup to cover a bad skin . . . pearl and diamond earrings and a gold and silver chain with a diamond at the center. She loves music, especially "song," and has traveled to concerts in Yugoslavia and Vienna. We discuss with mother and daughter the hard life of a ballerina. Elisabetta's decision to forswear it and become a schoolteacher did not displease her father.

We don't order from a menu—they bring course after course they think may please us. The owner knows Renato . . . everyone seems to know Renato. The meal begins with thin slices of fish in butter sauce. This is followed by *risotto con pesce, fritto misto,* beans—*pinto in olio*—and small shrimps—*gamberi*—with onions. There is ravioli colored with squid ink, filled with cheese and covered with butter sauce. There is fish on a bed of lettuce. Then comes a big platter of lobsters and giant shrimps. Finally there are chocolates, fruit, pastry, and coffee.

We talk about the article in a local newspaper about the Barsanti "dynasty," the leading family of Viareggio and what public benefactors they are. Besides the ambulance and dialysis machines there is the Villa Borbone with its surrounding acres that used to belong to the royal family of Austria, and came into the hands of the Barsantis. The villa has recently been donated to the Commune of Viareggio to be used for cultural purposes, but it seems that the various cultural organizations cannot agree how it should be used. In this, as in all matters pertaining to the "dynasty," there are legal complications.

Another complication is the beach property, Antaura, Principe, and so on. It has been discovered that the

144

grandfather left it to be divided equally among the grandchildren, but it was appropriated in its entirety by Giorgio. Giorgio is now being compelled to disgorge the part that does not belong to him. Anyone who thinks it's easy to be rich is mistaken.

At one point I mention that I was in Europe during the war, in the American army. This draws blank looks from l'Avvocato and his wife and daughter. People don't talk about the war, they'd rather forget it. It doesn't bear looking into . . . what your relatives were doing at the time. And there was no pastry to be had, no *gamberi.* The war was *brutto,* like bad weather, and now the sun is shining.

6/26

Read to Rosalind in the morning from Russell Baker's *Growing Up.* I had never read it and was dismayed to find that the opening chapter was about his aged mother who had a fall and was in a hospital. She was senile and thought she was living in the past.

My mother's old age is different: she is far from senile—she has all her faculties but talks obsessively of the past, telling the same stories over and over again.

We hear again about her coming to Venezuela. She was traveling for Helena Rubinstein with a $5000 letter of credit—she made them give it to her—and was in Caracas visiting important people. This was in 1945; the place was beautiful and, like pioneer country in the United States, undeveloped. She wasn't getting any younger—she was still attractive but a day would come when she wasn't. So she wired Rubenstein that she was coming to see them.

They urged her not to . . . thought she had taken leave of her senses. When she arrived by Clipper Madame Rubinstein refused to see her, but she persisted, and Madame finally consented. Rosalind had written out her plan on one page, and she gave it to Madame saying, "Please read this, and if you don't agree let's forget the matter." Madame read it and gave her the exclusive rights to sell Helena Rubinstein cosmetics in Venezuela.

She purchased an old building. She went from one drugstore to another selling Rubinstein products. The business grew until she had nineteen people working for her. Renato was sent by an Italian acquaintance they had in common. Renato was working for a beer company but they didn't like him because he wouldn't carry pencils in his shirt.

She and Renato didn't want a hole-and-corner relationship or, as it is described in Venezuela, "from one floor to another." So they were married, though it's almost impossible for an Italian man to bring himself to marry. They are fearful of being tied down.

They came to his part of Italy . . . Tuscany. She had always wanted "something special" in her life, and they bought the villa at San Alessio.

She talked, as she has many times, about renovating and furnishing Villa Rosalinda. I thought what a passion she has for furnishings . . . chairs, tables, mirrors, and carpets. I used to think this was terrible, but now I'm not

146

so sure. She has told me how in Russia, when she was a child, she took cardboard boxes and furnished the cellar where she slept.

The cellar was divided by a curtain—on the other side her older sister Lisa slept with her husband. She would hear them whispering in the night. And there were rats scurrying in the wall. Sometimes they ran across the floor.

She slept across three chairs. While she slept they would slide apart and she would fall to the floor. She picked up the bedclothes, pushed the chairs together, and climbed back.

Today is Sunday. There are more people than usual on the beach and the restaurant is crowded. We talk about life . . . these days at the villa incline one to do so. I say that the things we remember about people are not the things they pride themselves on, but some small incident, or something they said. Miriam remarks that it could be something unpleasant.

I remember, when I came to see Bly by train, his asking me, "Did you meet a widder-woman?"

Widder-woman? In Minnesota in the old days a widder-woman was hot stuff, like a "divorcée" in the thirties. Robert said it with the expression of a hick meeting a man from the big city, a knowing look . . . *We know what a feller like you gets up to on the road!*

George Ade knew: "Upon entering a Parlor Car at St. Paul he would select a Chair next to the Most Promising One in Sight, and ask her if she cared to have the Shade lowered.

Before the Train cleared the Yards he would have the Porter bringing a Foot-stool for the Lady. . . ."

The people in the street this evening are different, Miriam remarks . . . country people, couples, and families looking awkward in their Sunday clothes. They are all shapes and sizes . . . here and there some member of the family with a limp or a hanging lip. Farm workers in suits that are too tight, housemaids on their day off dressed to kill, "toughs" who push into you without apologizing . . . the street is theirs on Sunday evening. The tourists you see strolling on week nights are swallowed in the crowd of Sunday visitors, "villeggianti della domènica."

6/27

We've been worrying about our table. It's too long by ten centimeters . . . overwhelming in our living room.

Rosalind says you must never change an order once you've given it . . . this makes for confusion. It's one of her rules from experience. We decide to change it anyway, but not trust to the telephone—we drive to Pietrasanta again and see the manager change the specifications with his own hand.

Shopping in Viareggio . . . Miriam buys a dress at Max Mara for L145,000 or $108. The dress is brown; she thinks that brown doesn't go with her coloring, but this is lively with some red in it.

We buy two crystal vases, one to be given to Vincenza when we leave for her help in negotiating the table.

Grazia has admired Miriam's raincoat, so she is going to give it to her, and we spend some time going from store to store looking for a blouse for Grazia in addition. We shall give money to Giovanna, the woman who did our laundry and went so far as to press my underwear.

We are lying on the beach. Miriam is reading *The Dhammapada* and I am reading a detective story. The man goes by with his imitation Louis Vuitton bags. The ice-cream man passes, and the man who sells slices of coconut.

When we return to the villa I explore the disused third floor, looking for phonograph records. At the Villa Rosalinda, before Rosalind and Renato moved here, there were albums of fox-trots and musicals. And opera selections . . . when she was a girl Rosalind wanted to be a *prima donna.*

I don't find records but there are suitcases filled with odds and ends brought from San Alessio. There's a smell of moldy leather. One suitcase contains photographs . . . a studio photograph of Rosalind as a girl, when she wanted to be in opera. Or perhaps when she was an extra in motion pictures. She is looking up and to her right, hands raised behind her head with open palms. She appears to be dancing.

A photograph of Rosalind de Marantz having lunch with Helena Rubinstein . . . each has a plate of salad in front of her. There is a story to go with the salad. The company was promoting a diet that featured salads. They put a big plate of salad in front of Madame Rubinstein and a smaller portion in front of Miss de Marantz as befitted her position. Just before the shutter clicked

Madame switched plates so that the bigger portion appears in front of Miss de Marantz. The expression on Madame's face, turned toward the camera, is of one who has her wits about her and is up to all their tricks. If anyone is going to be made to look like a hearty feeder it isn't she!

There is a picture of my brother Herbert and myself in Jamaica. I must be about four, Herbert is five years older. We are sitting together on one chair, Herbert holding me around the waist.

I show Miriam the picture and she says I haven't changed—there's the same expression. I think it's what Jake Barnes called a look of "eager, deserving expectation."

6/29

I am writing this on the plane at Malpensa—name of ill omen!—while waiting to take off. The flight from Pisa to Rome was delayed and we had to go by way of Milan instead, and by taxi through Milan to Malpensa. No one told us when we arrived in Milan that there was a bus to take passengers to Malpensa. This little diversion by taxi for two hours through Milan cost L100,000, not to mention a L5000 gratuity for the driver.

Yesterday we had a long talk with Rosalind, saddened by the knowledge that it might be the last. She is stronger than she was two weeks ago, and the *prurito* has stopped more or less, but she is ninety-two or -three. Her age is a mystery she has guarded over the years. When she worked for Elizabeth Arden and Helena Rubinstein she took years off her age. Once she even altered her passport. Recently this got her into difficulties with Medicare when she wanted to collect some money due her—the age they had for her in their records varied. She said, "Do you think I could have done business in South America if they had known my real age? Those people put your age in the newspaper!"

She talked about affection being the most important thing of all. The reason she had worked so hard, driving herself, was that she did not have a companion. (I discussed this with Miriam later. She said that Rosalind was in the position of the teacher who marries a student. Renato was her employee when she married him, so she doesn't regard him as her equal.)

We were drinking tea, and she talked about drinking it in the Russian manner with a piece of sugar in the mouth. Miriam's father, who came from the same part of Russia, used to drink tea in the same way. There were some lines of a song Rosalind remembered from her childhood. Apparently tea was a rare luxury at one time.

"Tea," says the Captain and hands me a packet,
"This here is tea, I want you to make it . . ."

She talked about reading Tolstoy and Dostoyevsky. . . . As she talked there were flashes of the person she used to be.

Miriam and I had our last dinner in Viareggio at Ristorante Montecatini, *al fresco* in the garden. She had the *fileto Toscano classico* and I the *fritto misto . . .* to wipe out that damned Cohen. The day before I had eaten *fritto misto* in a third-rate restaurant.

During the night it thundered and lightened. Miriam says I made war noises in my sleep as I sometimes do. One night, early in our marriage, I projected a whole scenario, the sounds coming from different parts of the room. It was eery and she was thoroughly mystified.

The plane, a big 747, has taken off and we are above the clouds with the plains of Lombardy below, a patchwork of square fields and some that are not so square, colored brown and green. There are straight roads and villages with red roofs . . . to the left a broad, winding river. Now we have crossed the river and it lies behind us. The clouds have broken into puffballs with airy spaces between.

We are still climbing, for the houses are no longer distinctly separate and the fields have shrunk. A few minutes and we are above a mass of white cloud; through breaks in the mass we see dark mountains patched and lined with snow, and green slopes and valleys.

Loth to believe what we so grieved to hear,
For still we had hopes that pointed to the clouds,
We questioned him again, and yet again;
But every word that from the peasant's lips
Came in reply, translated by our feelings,
Ended in this,—*that we had crossed the Alps.*

In one of the old suitcases on the third floor there was a copy of Dostoyevsky . . . "White Nights" and "Notes from Underground." The first is all talk and a ridiculous story. "Notes from Underground" isn't a story, it reads like philosophy. I seem to recall that Saul Bellow was much taken with it at one time.

But who cares about the ramblings of "a sick man . . . a mean man"? And his philosophizing doesn't add up to much. "And so in the end, ladies and gentlemen, it's best to do nothing at all!" This may have been provocative in 1864 but no one needs to hear it now. The introduction says that Dostoyevsky was irritated with nineteenth-century ideas of Progress, with reason, socialist utopias, and the Crystal Palace. But in the twentieth century we hardly need to be told that Progress has its limits.

He heaps scorn on those who "reach out for the Absolute through aesthetics by claiming to 'devote their lives to the good and the beautiful.'" He needn't have bothered—nobody believes in the Absolute these days, and goodness and beauty have long been out of fashion.

Maybe Part Two will be better.

Yes. His wanting to make the officer step out of his way. Dressing up for a confrontation with the officer and, at the last moment, stepping aside. Bumping into him and being ignored.

The party where he is not wanted and to which he invites himself, and the way he is humiliated and abases himself . . . all this is too convincing. It's painful to read. I put the book aside for another time.

The voice of the captain informs us that we are an hour and fifty minutes from New York. Below us there is a flotilla of white clouds, and the blue sea far below.

If I were a novelist I would write about my mother's life. You would have to concentrate on certain episodes otherwise the thing would spread out in every direction. Where to begin? When the brick factory that her father owned burned down and he left for America? When Lisa died of typhus and she almost died too?

The widow, Pearl, took three children with her to New York, leaving Rosalind in charge of the two youngest, to follow later. She was twelve or thirteen years old. How slowly the days and nights pass when you are waiting to go to America! She had taught herself to read— there was no schooling for such as she in Russia in those days.

She worked in a factory in Manhattan. The family lived in Brooklyn and she had to get up early to get to work on time or lose her job.

A man was standing at the street door, talking to the women as they came out. Would she like to act in motion pictures?

Would she! She took the ferry to New Jersey where the studios were, at Fort Lee, and stood in line with other hopefuls. She was given bit parts, and one day when the leading actress refused to jump from a bridge into a tank of water she took her place and jumped. They had to pull her out—she couldn't swim. After that she took swimming lessons.

She took dance lessons, riding lessons in Central Park, and acting lessons on 42nd Street with Mr. Koppel and Van der Loop. She went to the theatrical agencies and the Fox studio in New York. Then there was an opening:

Fox was hiring girls to be mermaids in a picture featuring Annette Kellerman.

In Jamaica when you were a child she would take you with her on the afternoons when she drove to the Liguanea Club. She made you crouch in a bunker, keeping your head down while she swung at the ball.

She strode on ahead, the caddy following with the bag. The golf course was close to the hills. You could see them clearly with gullies running down their sides. A breeze had sprung up, rustling the leaves. It came from the sea and all the places in the world.